Praise for Sales Flashpoint

"Harris and Dickerson lay out an elegant yet simple game plan for creating and driving a high-performing sales team. This is an essential guide that should be referred to over and over again for anyone who wants to elevate their game. I wish I had this years ago when I first got started."
—Brennan Marilla, Vice President, US Sales, Medtronic Endovascular

"A well-researched book, packed with strategies and tactics that can be implemented and will move the needle quickly—regardless of the industry in which you sell. A must read!"
—Tom Nightingale, Vice President, Communications and Chief Marketing Officer, Con-way, Inc.

"Richard Dickerson and JK Harris have strategically mapped out a blueprint for higher sales achievement in Sales Flashpoint. Their common sense approach combined with their time-tested sales methodology provides the competitive edge every sales manager needs to have in the line of fire. No sales professional should be without a copy of Sales Flashpoint in their repertoire of sales training tools."
—Harvey Shapiro, District Sales Manager, Chase Auto Finance

"Every effective sales manager has a strategy or roadmap they used to become successful. This book gives you insight into developing and implementing that strategy for yourself, and does it in a way that is easy to understand and highly effective. This is a must-read for those that want to ultimately build and manage successful sales teams no matter what industry they are in."
—Corey Epperly, Vice President, Sales and Marketing, Personified, A CareerBuilder Company

"If sales is an art, Harris and Dickerson are true artists. They not only understand the process, they know how to make it work effectively. Add creativity to the formula and you have a 'must-read' book for anyone who wants to be a successful sales professional."

—Bruce Freeman, The Small Business Professor®, author and syndicated columnist

"I'm so grateful to John and Richard for creating a book that not only reinforces some classic sales lessons, but also provides insight into new strategies to help me and my sales team 'turn up the heat.' Our business requires face-to-face, 'get it done' sales interactions with new prospects every day, and Sales Flashpoint *has helped me sharpen my sales saw, for sure! Definitely one to keep and carry with me."*

—Andy S. Albright, President & CEO, National Agents Alliance

"This is the instruction manual for sales managers. Richard Dickerson and JK Harris have identified the challenges and offered the solutions. Every sales manager should study and use Sales Flashpoint *as their guide to hire and develop a world-class sales force. Excellent resource!"*

—Veronica Fogelman, Owner/Principal, Ledgerock Consulting

"Imagine being offered the tools to hire a better sales force and train them to promote and sell your products more effectively. Whether you're a CEO or an entrepreneur, Sales Flashpoint *should be your primer."*

—Dave Feltovic, President, Weatherproof Systems, Inc.

"Understanding how to choose the right people for the job is critical to building a successful sales team. The whole person assessment is the key that will help you take your company to the Flashpoint."

—Laurie St. Pierre, RN, BSN, Senior Case Manager, HCR Manor Care

sales
flashpoint

FIFTEEN STRATEGIES FOR RAPID-FIRE SALES GROWTH

Hire
Train
Manage

JK Harris and Richard D. Dickerson

EP
Entrepreneur.
Press

Jere L. Calmes, Publisher
Cover design: Desktop Miracles
Composition and production: Eliot House Productions

This publication is designed to provide accurate and authoritative information in regard to the subject matter covered. It is sold with the understanding that the publisher is not engaged in rendering legal, accounting, or
other professional services. If legal advice or other expert assistance is
required, the services of a competent professional person should be sought.

Library of Congress Cataloging-in-Publication Data
    Harris, JK
    Sales flashpoint: fifteen strategies for rapid-fire sales growth/by JK
Harris and Richard D. Dickerson.
       p.   cm.
    ISBN-13: 978-1-59918-388-6 (alk. paper)
    ISBN-10: 1-59918-388-9
    1. Sales management. 2. Selling. 3. Sales personnel. I. Dickerson,
Richard. II. Title.
    HF5438.4.H367 2010
      658.8'101—dc22   2010006663

Printed in the United States of America

14 13 12 11   10 9 8 7 6 5 4 3 2 1

In Memory of
William T. "Bill" Brooks

Contents

part two

Train Right

part three

Manage Right

Acknowledgments

There's a risk to attempting to acknowledge all the people who helped us take an idea and turn it into the book that is now in your hands, and that is that there were so many, we're likely to leave some out. We want to take that risk because we think it's important to let those who contributed to this project know how much we appreciate what they did. And if we inadvertently overlook someone, we apologize in advance.

From JK Harris

I am eternally grateful to the late Bill Brooks, to whom this book is dedicated. His insight and understanding of human nature and his ability to translate that into strategies companies can use to create powerful sales teams have had a positive impact on thousands of

organizations over the years—none more than JK Harris & Company. Bill was able to understand me and work with my personality. He reintroduced me to the value of whole person assessments and showed me how to use them to drive the growth of my company. I am now committed to sharing his message and methods with other entrepreneurs and business managers.

Certainly everyone on the JK Harris & Company team contributed to this book by virtue of their contributions to the company. In particular, for their roles in successfully implementing the strategies in *Sales Flashpoint*, I'd like to recognize Bob Harris, my brother, who is the executive vice president of operations; Gene Graham, our executive vice president of sales and marketing; Oscar Luykenaar, our chief financial officer; and Mark Monaghan, senior vice president of human resources.

I'd also like to thank the team at Entrepreneur Press for their support and guidance. I appreciate the wisdom of Jere Calmes, publisher. I especially want to thank Leanne Harvey and Jillian McTigue for their contributions to the marketing process and for coming up with the concept that became the Flashpoints brand. Marla Markman did a great job editing the manuscript; Karen Billipp and Eliot House Productions carried that work through to the final design; and Barry Kerrigan and Del LeMond of Desktop Miracles did another striking job on the cover.

Finally, special thanks to Jacquelyn Lynn for her ability to capture our message and put it into an organized, easy-to-read presentation and for her relentless insistence that Richard and I stay on track and on message as we worked.

From Richard D. Dickerson

I chose to dedicate this book to Bill Brooks, who saw potential in me, brought me into his company, encouraged me to excel and develop my craft, and demonstrated the way.

To all my colleagues and loyal clients over the years, thank you for your support and patience. I appreciate each of you.

Thanks to my friend, client, and co-author John Harris, who saw value in my partnership in writing this book. And, of course, to Jacquelyn Lynn, for her untiring work and incredible patience, without whom this book would never have come to fruition.

Notes from the Authors

We wrote this book together and for the most part speak in the plural first person. On the occasions where a particular story is being told by one of us, we use the singular first person and indicate who is speaking in parentheses.

All the anecdotes in this book are true. In most cases, the names have been either eliminated or changed to protect the innocent, the guilty, and the not-too-smart.

Preface

If you know anything about business, you know these realities:

1. Everything starts with marketing and sales.
2. Nothing happens until someone sells something.
3. No product is so good that it sells itself.
4. If the "better mousetrap" theory was ever true, it isn't any-more—and it won't ever be again.

Companies that are successful today and will be successful in the future are sales-driven organizations. Their leaders understand the need to reach and surpass the Sales Flashpoint—and to do it every day, over and over, at every opportunity.

Organizations that are not sales-driven will not survive long. This is true whether you have a single hot dog cart or are a behemoth like Walmart or Microsoft. In fact, even if you are far and away the top dog in your industry, you can't just sit around. You have to continuously innovate and sell those innovations to the market.

Most entrepreneurs don't have a problem with the innovation side of things. It's their nature to always be coming up with new ideas and better ways of doing things. But many entrepreneurs—in fact, many people—have a problem with the sales side of business.

One of the key reasons we decided to write this book is to spread the message that "sell" is *not* a four-letter word. We know that over the years, sales has developed a bad reputation in many arenas—and in some cases, that reputation is well-deserved. We also know that sales is an honorable profession that is an essential component of business success. Yes, there are some salespeople who lack skill, some who think pressure works better than persuasion, and some whose ethics are questionable. But those statements can be applied to every profession because they are a representation of human nature. And the fact that there are some not-so-great salespeople in the world shouldn't stop you from working to take your sales team to the Flashpoint. On the contrary, it should motivate you to build the most effective and professional sales force in your industry.

With that said, we must also stress that this is not a "how to sell" book. We will discuss basic selling skills, but we'll do it within the larger context of hiring the right people, training them, and managing them effectively. We know from experience that sales techniques alone are not enough to make a sales team successful. If you hire salespeople who aren't right for your product, your company, and your culture, there is no way they can be more than mediocre, no matter how skilled they may be. If you don't effectively manage your sales team, they won't reach their full potential. And if there is not a viable sales culture—that is, one that supports sales and proactively seeks to eliminate obstacles— within your organization, generating revenue will be a struggle.

But if you hire, train, and manage according to the strategies we outline in this book, you will have a winning sales team.

One important caveat is that these 15 strategies work together, building on one another. If you are going to reach the Sales Flashpoint, you need to understand and apply all 15 strategies. This is not an a la carte menu. You can't pick and choose the ones you think might be easy and ignore the ones that will take more effort. If you do, you might see a slight improvement in your sales, but you won't reach the Flashpoint. Make the commitment to all 15 strategies—and watch your sales skyrocket.

We've seen it happen again and again, and the reason is simple: The strategies in *Sales Flashpoint* are based on solid principles. Because they are principle-based, they are timeless. Markets may change. Technology will definitely change. But these 15 strategies will work today, tomorrow, and decades from now.

Join us now on this immensely rewarding journey as we help you take your company to the Sales Flashpoint.

—JK Harris
Richard D. Dickerson

The Best Way to Read *Sales Flashpoint*

Effective reading isn't a passive activity. To truly benefit from the time and money you've invested, read actively. Keep a pen and highlighter nearby; mark passages of special interest to you, and jot ideas in the margins. Write down how you can use the strategies as you think of them so you don't forget. Dog-ear the pages, or use stick-on tabs so you can easily find your notes later. Talk to others about what you've read. Most important, when you've finished the book, don't just put it back on the shelf—take action, and use what you've learned.

Sales Flashpoint: Fifteen Strategies for Rapid-Fire Sales Growth is packed with valuable information for entrepreneurs, sales managers, and salespeople—get the most out of it.

Flashpoint

noun

1. The lowest temperature at which the vapor of a combustible liquid can be made to ignite momentarily in air

2. A point at which someone or something bursts into significant action or creation

part one

Hire Right

The first step in building a sales team that will take you to the Flashpoint is to hire the right people. While that sounds simple, so does the advice that if you want to lose weight, you should reduce the amount of food you eat. The good news is that hiring the right people is a lot easier to actually do than sticking to a diet, and you're going to learn how to do that in the first three strategies.

Your people are the foundation of your sales team. If they are not a good fit for sales in general and your company in particular, they will never be able to perform beyond a mediocre level—they will never reach the Sales Flashpoint.

Hiring the right people in any capacity is important—in sales, it is absolutely critical. Here's how you do it.

Hire the Whole Person

To make good hiring decisions, you need to know who you are hiring. By knowing them, we don't mean knowing their favorite color or ice cream flavor, or what they like to read, or whether they like sports or the opera. We mean knowing how they will perform on the job, why they will do it, if they will do the job, and whether or not they have the skills necessary to do it. Think about it from this perspective: If eating whole foods is good for your body, hiring the whole person—not just a part that you saw in an interview or on a resume—is good for your company.

Some of this information will be revealed through applications, resumes, and interviews, but to get a true, accurate, and complete picture of the candidate, to find out who the whole person is, you need to use proven assessment tools.

Key Measurements

There are four key areas you need to assess in a candidate: How, why, will, and can. All four areas work in concert to create a high achiever who will be right for your team.

Note that the issue of *can*—that is, the actual skills necessary for the job—is last on the list. Yes, those skills are important, but other factors are more critical. Consider that Michael Jordan and Dennis Rodman are both great basketball players, but which one do you want on your team? If you had to choose between football players Jerry Rice and Terrell Owens, who would you choose to represent your company? Or skaters Michelle Kwan and Tonya Harding?

Research has shown that people are often hired based primarily on their job or professional skills, but when they are fired, it's

Get to Know Yourself

If you have never taken an assessment (note that these are not tests, although they have the look and feel of one), or even if you have, it's a good idea to do it as part of the process of implementing a whole person assessment strategy. You should understand yourself at least as well as you want to understand the people you are considering hiring. What's more, going through the process will make you more comfortable with asking others to do it and give you more confidence in the results.

You may be surprised at how accurately a quality whole person assessment tool can identify your behavior styles, attitudes, motivations, and values. It can confirm what you know about yourself and often help you understand certain aspects of yourself that you may not have previously given a lot of thought to. It will also increase your own trust in the process. And once you have that information in a clearly articulated format, you can use it for your own personal and professional development.

usually because of personal skills or attributes. The receptionist who is attractive, friendly, and able to juggle busy phones and demanding in-person visitors with aplomb is considered a great hire—until she demonstrates that she can't get to work or back from

> *"If you're going to perform at a top level, you need to know who you are."*
> —JK Harris

lunch on time. The graphic designer who does beautiful work but never meets a deadline will frustrate everyone in the production chain and will likely end up being replaced. The manager who gets the job done but does so with degrading remarks about other employees will eventually damage morale to the extent that termination is the only option. These people all had the right professional skills, but they were clearly hiring mistakes that could have been avoided.

Let's take a look at each key area in more detail.

How Will They Do the Job?

The question of how people will do the job is answered in their basic behaviors. The four general behavioral dimensions are assertion, relativeness, systemization, and accuracy. You may be more familiar with this described as DISC, which is a four-quadrant behavioral model based on the work of William Moulton Marston, Ph.D., and used to examine the behavior of individuals in their environment or within a specific situation. DISC is an acronym for dominance (relating to control, power, and assertiveness), influence (relating to social situations and communication), steadiness (relating to patience, persistence, and thoughtfulness), and conscientiousness (relating to structure and organization).

We use the model developed by The Brooks Group and Target Training International (TTI), which categorizes behavioral styles as doer (directs others), talker (relates to others), pacer (accommodates others), and controller (assesses others). There are two basic types of behavioral styles: natural, which is what the person would do without any external influence, and adaptive, which is the individual's behavior in response to his environment. For example, someone's natural style may be introverted and solitary, but the adaptive style is extroverted and gregarious. Or the natural style may be to drink cheap beer, but at a business dinner, the adaptive style is to either not drink at all or consume high-end brand-name liquor. Or the natural style may be messy, disorganized, and always tardy, but the adaptive style is neat, organized, and punctual. Though we haven't administered an assessment to U.S. Federal Reserve Chairman Ben Bernanke, we believe he is a classic example whose natural style is introverted and analytical, but his adaptive style is outgoing and relative. You probably know people who are like this, or who change their behavior in other ways as the situation requires.

We all have the ability to adapt our style to some degree to the environment. People will adjust their behavior to what they believe the environment requires, and they can often do it very well. One of the things a good assessment tool will measure is an individual's willingness to be adaptive, which is something you should know before you make a hiring decision.

When you understand an individual's natural and adaptive styles, you can predict how they will do what they do. But you need to keep in mind that it's possible to hire someone whose natural style is not a fit for your organization but whose adaptive style is, so they will do well. In general, it is easier for high-energy people to tone down than it is for low-energy people to boost up, although both can be done. But the problem is that when human beings are under stress, pressure, or fatigue, we resort to our natural style. We simply cannot handle high levels of stress and anxiety and at the same time adapt our behavior to a style that is not natural for us. Unfortunately, many of the assessment tools on the market only measure adaptive styles. When you hire based on adaptive style without knowing and understanding the individual's natural style and then the person resorts to his natural style to deal with a stressful situation, you're confused by what you see as totally unpredicted behavior.

> *"You can buy a person's hands, but you can't buy his heart. His heart is where his enthusiasm, his loyalty is."*
> —Stephen Covey

There is no hard and fast rule that a good salesperson should fit a certain behavior model. For example, it's commonly assumed that the top salespeople are extroverts, and certainly many of them are. But we have seen plenty of introverts who have been very successful salespeople in the appropriate culture. It's easier to do certain jobs successfully if you have the appropriate behavior styles, but not having those precise styles shouldn't be an automatic disqualification. Every person is a blend of all four behavioral styles, with some being more dominant than others. The very best salespeople are so adaptive that they recognize the buyer's style and mirror it.

Why Will They Do the Job?

Why someone will do a job is based on their values and motivations. It's human nature to look for cultures that support, reward, and condone our internal motivators. If you're excited by making money, you'll seek an environment that can fulfill your desire for money and monetary things. If you're motivated by helping other people, you'll seek an environment that will provide opportunities for serving and nurturing. And if you can't find a job that fulfills your values and motivations, you'll seek that fulfillment elsewhere, such as in an avocation or hobby.

While most salespeople are motivated by economic rewards, not all are—and for many, the motivation to make money is driven more by what they want to do with that money than the money itself. Some may desire money to fund an opulent lifestyle; for others, the need to make money is driven by the desire to ensure financial security or give to charitable causes.

You need to know what motivates your salespeople because if what motivates them is not supported, rewarded, and condoned in your culture, they will not be energized and, consequently, they will not perform at their peak level.

There are six basic internal drivers: knowledge, money, beauty, people, power, and tradition. Let's take a brief look at each of them.

Knowledge is essentially a zeal for learning. People who are driven by knowledge just love to learn. They want to know for the sake of knowing. The money driver is based on money and material possessions. People who are driven by money are energized by financial goals. They may or may not care about accumulating money; some just use it as a scorecard of their personal success, and they may spend it or give it away as fast as they make it. People who are driven by beauty are passionate about their surroundings. They like things to be pretty, they care about colors, textures, and the stability of their environment. They want things to be in harmony, calm, and predictable. Those with a strong people driver have a passion for the welfare of others. They are highly sympathetic, often social crusaders. They are willing to give and assist, sometimes even to their own detriment. Others may be very empathetic, understanding how someone else feels without taking on those feelings. People with a strong power driver are passionate about being seen as a leader, as someone who is influential. They want to be in charge of their own destiny and often the destiny of others. Tradition-driven people have a passion for doing the right thing and a very strong and deep belief system about how life should be lived. Everyone has all six of those drivers, with some being more dominant than others.

Values drive our behaviors, which is the reason an individual's top three drivers will dominate why he performs. He will seek out cultures that will reward and support those drivers. If he can't find a workplace culture that fulfills his values, he may settle for something else and fulfill those drivers with hobbies and social activities. That's a reason you need to look at the whole person—one of the ways to identify potential top performers is to look at what people do in their off-work hours. Do they enjoy highly competitive activities? If you're looking for someone with a highly competitive nature, this is a good sign. Do they do a lot of volunteer work? If you want your salespeople to build long-term, nurturing relationships with clients, this would be something you should look for.

> "Never permit a dichotomy to rule your life, a dichotomy in which you hate what you do so you can have pleasure in your spare time. Look for a situation in which your work will give you as much happiness as your spare time."
>
> —Edward L. Bernays

Keep in mind that a hobby can relate to a person's engagement on the job. If, for example, an individual is not in a workplace culture that fulfills his values and he turns to a recreational activity for that fulfillment, he may spend time on the job thinking about where he would prefer to be instead. You don't want that person. You want people who will perform at their peak because they are motivated by the job, not who will do the job simply because they need the money so they can pay their bills and be able to spend their time after hours doing the things they're really excited about.

Will They Do the Job?

The will question is answered by their personal attitudes and skills, which determine if they are willing to perform. Is their perception of sales as a career positive? Do they have the discipline to get up and do what is necessary to be successful every day? What do they see as being important, and how clearly do they see it? We

> *"Most people have fairly well-developed sales skills. They know how to sell, and they use those skills all the time in their various relationships. But they are not successful professional salespeople because they don't want to be called 'salespeople.' It's about how they see themselves. "*
>
> —Richard D. Dickerson

call this cognitive perception, or attitude. It is the accelerator or decelerator of performance.

The "will" part of doing a job boils down to clarity and focus. They know what's important, and they've put a spotlight on it, and they are willing to develop the personal skills necessary to accomplish it. By personal skills, we mean things like personal accountability, goal-setting, realistic expectations, the ability to relate to others, persistence, even something as basic as good manners. In fact, sales careers are rarely ended by a lack of technical, job, or sales skills—they are ended by a lack of personal skills. We can teach the job and sales skills, but we can only refine the personal skills—we can't change them. Be sure the people you hire have the personal skills that will make them willing to perform in your environment.

Can They Do the Job?

The "can" part of the equation deals with their professional skills. Do they know how to prospect, research potential customers, prepare for a sales call, make a presentation, answer questions, and close the sale?

In Strategy Three, we will discuss how to benchmark a job, and a key part of the benchmark is defining the skills necessary to succeed in the position. You need to compare the candidate's professional skills and potential with the benchmarks of the position to determine if he can actually do the job.

The Instruction Manual for People

Would you buy a piece of office or production equipment without a manual to tell you how to operate and maintain it? Of course not. Yet every day, companies hire people who are far more complex than any machine, cost more than machines, and produce far more revenue than any machine possibly could—but don't even consider trying to understand how they work and what they need to stay in top form.

Whole person assessments are the instruction and operations manual for your employees. These tools tell you who you are hiring, how they function, what motivates them, and whether or not they can actually do the job. Once people are hired, assessments become tools for managing, directing career paths, helping employees reach their peak performance—essentially, assessments are your employee coaching manual and a life manual for your people.

The Interview

Interviews will always be an essential part of the hiring process, but they should come after the assessment, not before or instead of. Use a validated whole person assessment to identify your top candidates and weed out the people who just aren't right for your company, then to guide the interview with the people who are strong candidates so you can make the best final choice.

No matter how intuitive you are or how good of a judge of character you think you are, the reality is that people can fool you, but they can't fool these assessment tools. What's more, the

> "Hire slowly and with caution. Fire with dispatch."
> —Richard D. Dickerson

assessment can often tell you things about people that they can't articulate about themselves. You can use the assessment results to generate interview questions that will confirm and expand on what the assessment told you.

How to Conduct a Successful Sales Interview

You need solid answers to four basic questions before you extend an offer:

1. How will this person sell?
2. Why would this person choose to sell?
3. Will this person sell?
4. Can this person sell?

To get the answers you need, you should investigate these five areas:

1. *What they know*. This includes education, work experience, skills, training, aptitudes, and equivalent experience. What in their background has prepared them to be an asset or a liability for you and your organization?

   As part of this process, conduct a thorough background check. Verify everything the prospective salesperson claims. Call the references. Don't assume that applicants will only include references that will give them glowing recommendations; you may be surprised at what some references will reveal. Studies show that nearly one-fourth of all resumes have blatant lies on them, and 98 percent of those resumes are from people applying for sales jobs. Whether or not you choose to hire someone who has lied on a resume is your call—although we don't recommend it—but before you can make that decision, you need to know.

2. *What they are likely to do*. This is answered by their behavior and personality traits. You want to know how they are likely to perform their job.

3. *Whether they will actually do it.* This is answered by their attitudes and personal skills. Look at how they relate to people, how they treat the interviewer, and how they respond to questions. Consider their speech patterns and word choices. Evaluate these issues both from the perspective of what they reveal about the person and also how well the person is likely to be a fit for the job and your culture.

> *"When love and skill work together, expect a masterpiece."*
> —John Ruskin

4. *Why they are likely to do it.* Remember the why is driven by personal interests and values. During the interview, look for indicators of what really excites them. Again, a good match between their values and your culture is critical.

5. *Where they must fit in.* Understand your own corporate and industry culture issues so that you can evaluate how well a candidate will fit. A starched-shirt, buttoned-down, suit-and-tie kind of person is simply not going to fit in a laid-back,

Should You Record Interviews?

Technology makes it easy and affordable to create a digital video recording of interviews for later review and sharing with people who were not able to participate in the actual interview. This can be especially useful if there is disagreement on your hiring team about a particular candidate; the video can be reviewed for clarification and additional discussion.

If you are going to record an interview, the candidate should be advised orally and in writing and should consent to the recording. Let the candidate know how you will use the recording, as well as how and when it will be destroyed. Never record a candidate without his knowledge and permission.

anything-goes kind of culture, no matter how experienced or skilled he is. And the laid-back, anything-goes kind of person isn't going to fit in the starched-shirt, buttoned-down, suit-and-tie culture. When people don't fit, they don't succeed.

Interviewing Tools

To really know who you are hiring, use a complete range of interviewing tools. Just using one or a few will not give you the whole picture of the applicant.

Your candidate evaluation process should consist of three relatively equal parts: 1) reviewing resumes and applications, conducting background checks, looking for the right qualifications; 2) multiple phone and face-to-face interviews in a variety of environments with different interviewers; and 3) an objective whole person assessment that will validate what you experienced with the background research and interviews. This will give you a complete picture that is both objective and subjective.

We recommend:

1. *Good, solid interview questions.* Make your questions open-ended in a style that encourages dialogue. Develop your questions ahead of time. You want to ask some standard questions of every applicant, but you also want to develop questions that are specific to each applicant based on the information you have about that person. Make the questions easy to understand and answer. An interview is not a battle of wits but a chance for you to get to know the candidate. Remember that the interviewee should do 95 percent of the talking.

   For example, you might ask, "What in your background has prepared you to be an asset to my organization?" Then be quiet and listen. You're interested in what they say, as well as in how they say it. You want to see how well they think on their feet. Listen to what's being "said" between their words.

2. *Follow-up questions to dig deeper.* Explore the candidate's responses. Once you've received an answer, ask a question around the response. Whenever possible, go at least three questions deep to get as much detail and clarity as possible.

3. *Multiple interviews and interviewers.* Put candidates in a variety of environments, such as in your office, on a facility tour, on the telephone, and even outside the office, as well as with a variety of interviewers, both one at a time and two, three, or even more at a time.

Preparing the Interviewers

Be sure the interviewers take their role seriously and are prepared. They are making major decisions that will have a tremendous impact on your company. They should understand the job and the culture, and be able to evaluate the candidate and offer their perceptions. They cannot be nervous or tense; such behaviors are clearly noticeable and can derail an interview.

A salesperson we know used to have a manager who, in the process of an interview, would snag anybody he could find in the office at the moment to sit down with the candidate. The interviewer didn't know anything about the candidate or what he had been told, and neither one really knew why they were talking to each other. Those "interviews" were totally unproductive, a waste of time, and absolutely useless to both the company and the candidate.

Work with the interviewers ahead of time so that they know the type and nature of questions they need to ask. They need to know the sort of information you're looking for so that they're paying attention to the right things and making the right notes. Provide them with questions based on the candidate's whole person assessment and the job's benchmark.

We recommend that at least one interview be over a meal with the candidate's significant other (spouse or non-married partner, if they have one) so you can evaluate the individual's personal skill development in a non-business or social setting. Watch how they interact with their significant other, the wait staff, and even other customers in the restaurant. Pay attention to how they order and how they eat—eating habits will tell you a lot. Do they order an alcoholic beverage? A drink or wine with dinner is fine, but a drink at lunch is a red flag. It shows a lack of respect for the host. When people relax in a social setting, they will tell you things that they may not reveal in a formal business environment. And most candidates will relax when you invite them to a meal because it's perceived as non-business.

When candidates can handle themselves well in a lunch or dinner interview, they can probably handle themselves in most any situation. Also, because many sales positions require that clients be entertained at meals and other social functions, you want to be sure a candidate will be comfortable with that part of the job.

4. *Testing and instrumentation.* These are the assessment tools that measure behavior, personal skills, and values—the tools that tell you who you are really dealing with. They are absolutely essential to making a sound hiring decision.

5. *Personal observation.* Every member of your interviewing team should record and report personal observations. Be sure the interview process is long enough to allow for meaningful observation.

6. *Background checks.* Look for a history of integrity. A background check will tell you if the candidate was honest when providing information on a resume and application. Consider the entire picture—education, references, civil

What Including the Spouse/Significant Other Can Tell You

Not all candidates will be married, engaged, or in committed, long-term relationships, but when they are, you want to meet their partner. The easiest and best way to do that is, after the candidate has passed the initial round of interviews, to say, "We'd like to have you and your significant other, should you have one, join us for dinner." Then allow them to respond.

If your company requires salespeople to entertain customers in various social settings, making that part of the interview process is critical. But even if your sales positions don't involve entertainment, taking a candidate to dinner with spouses/significant others (yours as well as theirs) can tell you a great deal. An individual's choice of mate tells you a lot about themselves. For example, you may have a candidate who is sharp and presents well, but the spouse is a slob. People tend to marry people who are a reflection of themselves, so do you want to hire that person? Maybe, maybe not. Or the candidate is bright and articulate, but the spouse uses poor grammar and foul language. If you expect your salespeople to entertain customers, this could be a problem.

Another reason to include spouses/partners in the interviewing process is that they often have a great deal of influence on a person's career choices. That's why you want the significant other to hear what the candidate hears, to be able to ask questions about the job and the company, and to be involved in the process.

court records, criminal record, driving record, credit history, drug use and so on—and don't let one negative be an automatic exclusion. For example, many top sales performers will have lousy driving records and spotty credit histories. If you automatically exclude these candidates, you may be doing your company a disservice. A better strategy is to put these negatives into context, discuss them with the candidate, and then make a decision.

7. *Listening.* Give your undivided attention to the candidate. Listen with your eyes, ears, heart, and soul. Don't be afraid of some silence. You want to focus on what the candidate is saying, not on what you're going to ask next, so you may need to pause between an answer and your next question. As you listen, pay attention to things like volume, tone, pace, and enunciation because these are important skills for a salesperson to have.

Interview Tips and Techniques

Top salespeople know that preparation is critical to sales success as well as making good hiring decisions.

Conduct interviews in the proper environment. The setting should be as neutral as possible, with no distractions or interruptions. Close the door, have your calls routed to voice mail, ignore your e-mail and text messages, and turn your cell phone off. When you allow interruptions, you are essentially telling the candidate that you don't think this meeting is very important.

Establish a relaxed atmosphere. Smile and be cordial. Introduce yourself, and call the applicant by name. Make consistent eye contact without staring. One of the best ways to do that is to focus on one eye of the other person so that your own eyes don't shift from side to side.

Arrange seating that is non-threatening. Your desk and office should be clean and neat—or, if space is available, consider holding the meeting in a small conference room. Do not use or allow use of tobacco products (most states have laws in place restricting indoor smoking in businesses and other public places); however, if it's convenient, have coffee or soft drinks.

Begin with small talk—the weather, the traffic, and so on. Then get the candidate comfortable answering your questions by asking about hobbies, activities, or interests before you move to more serious job-related topics.

Don't lead with information about you or your job. This telegraphs what you are looking for and may make the applicant more nervous. The basic information about the job should have already been provided with the job listing, and smart candidates will have already done their own research on your company. You want the candidate to be able to respond to your questions without being influenced by anything you've said. Certainly as the interview progresses, you'll provide additional information and offer the candidate an opportunity to ask questions, but don't do it upfront.

Use open-ended questions to get the candidate talking. These are very similar in style to the open-ended questions a top sales performer would use on a sales call, and include phrasing such as, "Tell me how you feel about . . ." and "Tell me about a time when you . . ."

During the course of the interview, look for clear indications that the applicant can and will sell—don't just take their word for it.

What Does It Cost When a Salesperson Underperforms or Fails?

If you're wondering if you can afford whole person assessments, either from a hard-cost or time-involved perspective, consider this: If the assessments prevent you from just one hiring mistake, they've paid for themselves—and they'll probably prevent many.

Use this worksheet to calculate the cost of a salesperson hiring mistake:

Salesperson Worksheet, continued

Advertising, recruiting, and interviewing expenses
for the mishired salesperson $_____

Advertising, recruiting, and interviewing expenses
to replace the mishired salesperson $_____

Failed salesperson's salary $_____

Failed salesperson's benefits $_____

Failed salesperson's training program and expenses $_____

Office equipment and supplies $_____

Prorated expense for office space $_____

Net profit on lost sales $_____

Wasted sales management time $_____

Wasted administrative time $_____

Time required for other salespeople to handle
failed salesperson's miscues $_____

Time other salespeople spent being distracted
by the situation $_____

Customers failed salesperson has alienated $_____

Prospects failed salesperson has alienated $_____

Loss of referrals from alienated customers and prospects $_____

Qualified prospects not properly handled by
failed salesperson $_____

Salesperson Worksheet, continued

Morale and other problems failed salesperson generated	$_____
Reimbursement for travel	$_____
Reimbursement for expenses	$_____
Wasted expense for related consumables, such as brochures, sales aids, postage, etc.	$_____
Special purchases, such as cell phone, laptop computer, vehicle, etc.	$_____
Time spent in worry, frustration, and anxiety	$_____
Executive and staff time involvement	$_____
Time spent in meetings dealing with problems and resolution	$_____
Costs of hiring another salesperson to replace failed salesperson	$_____
Legal fees for issues surrounding termination	$_____
Total:	$_____

No Placeholders Allowed

It is better to leave a position vacant than to put the wrong person in it. In the long run—and often even in the short run—it will cost you more to hire the wrong person than to wait for the right person.

An argument against this position is that at least the wrong person is doing *something* as opposed to nothing getting done. In the case of salespeople, at least they're out there making calls. But the flaw in that thinking is that you don't really know exactly what they're doing, and they could be doing more damage than good. Consider this scenario: You hire a person who is unsuited for sales in your culture because you haven't gotten any applicants you really like, and you want to get someone in the job. You find out about a prospective customer with significant potential, and you send this salesperson out to make a call—and he blows it. You could look at the situation and figure you're no worse off than before, but in fact you are. You not only don't have the immediate business that the salesperson failed to obtain, but you will find it more difficult in the future to sell that customer because he now has a negative instead of a neutral opinion of your company.

Don't hire placeholders. If you don't have the right person for the right job, leave the position open until you can find the right person.

—— KEY LESSONS ——

* Before you make a hiring decision, get to know the candidates from a whole person perspective.

* The four key areas you should assess in a candidate are how, why, will, and can they do the job.

* People are usually hired based on their professional skills but fired based on their personal skills.

* Be sure the people you hire have the personal skills that will make them willing to perform in your environment. Those skills include personal accountability, goal-setting, realistic expectations, the ability to relate to others, persistence, and even good manners.

* The two basic types of behavioral styles are natural, which is what we do without any external influence, and adaptive, which is our behavior in response to the environment. We are all adaptive to some degree.

* There is no rule that says a good salesperson should fit a certain behavior model.

* The six basic internal drivers are knowledge, money, beauty, people, power, and tradition. An individual's top three drivers will dominate how he performs. He will seek out cultures that will reward and support those drivers.

* In the hiring process, the assessment should be done before you conduct any interviews. This lets you identify top candidates so you don't waste time talking with people who aren't right for your organization.

* Before you extend an offer, you need to find out these key things about candidates: what they know, what they are likely to do, whether they will actually do it, why they are likely to do it, and where they will fit in your organization.

* Your hiring process should consist of three parts: 1) reviewing resumes and applications, conducting background checks, looking for the right qualifications; 2) multiple phone and face-to-face interviews; and 3) an objective whole person assessment.

* Interviewing tools should include good, solid questions with appropriate follow-up questions; multiple interviews and interviewers; testing and instrumentation; personal observation; background checks; and listening.

* Be sure all the interviewers take their role seriously and are prepared to evaluate the candidate and offer their perceptions.

* Conduct interviews in a neutral environment with no distractions or interruptions. Establish a relaxed atmosphere. Arrange

seating that is non-threatening. Use open-ended questions. Don't lead with information about the job; let the candidate respond to your questions first.

* When candidates are married or in a committed long-term relationship, you should meet their partner. The best way to do that is to invite them to dinner.

* Know what it costs you to make a hiring mistake on your sales team.

* If you don't have the right person for the job, leave the position open until you do.

Separate the Shining Stars from the Dim Bulbs

There's a lot more to identifying the top candidates than simply reviewing resumes and conducting background checks. The best way to know your candidates is with a whole person assessment, which can predict with remarkable accuracy how an individual will perform on the job.

How It All Began

As is often the case with research and development, one of the earliest applications of a true assessment came about by accident. In the 1920s, William Moulton Marston, the inventor of the systolic blood pressure test, which became a component of the modern polygraph, was looking for a way to validate the questions he used with his invention. The Harvard-educated college professor sent his graduate students out to public areas in major metropolitan areas like Boston and New York and told them to watch people and record what they saw. One of Marston's graduate assistants used the data those students collected to build the first application of a behavioral profile that could be validated by observation, an instrument that is credited to Marston and is still in use today: the DISC profile we discussed in Strategy One.

The intriguing and unconventional Marston lived in a polyamorous relationship with his wife and another woman, who happened to be one of his graduate assistants. He was a psychologist, feminist theorist, inventor, and the creator of the Wonder Woman comic book character under the pen name of Charles Moulton. Marston did not believe his attempts at lie detection were simply an application of technology but rather that interrogation techniques coupled with technology were how lies could be detected. Marston wanted to understand more than just how people behaved; he wanted to understand how their behavior changed from situation to situation. A goal of his research was to increase people's understanding of themselves while decreasing misunderstandings between individuals. Today, we can use his work to help companies reach the Sales Flashpoint.

During the late 1950s and early '60s, two Harvard professors spent seven years researching the characteristics that are necessary for a salesperson to be able to sell successfully. An article from that research, "What Makes a Good Salesman" by David Mayer and Herbert M. Greenberg, has been published twice in the *Harvard Business Review*. Mayer and Greenberg found two characteristics that were consistently present in those high achievers: healthy ego drive and empathetic outlook. That information was re-examined about a decade ago, and the results were the same: Top performing salespeople have healthy egos and empathetic outlooks.

In this context, a healthy ego drive means the salesperson has a personal want and need to make the sale. It's not just for the money. It's almost a conquest, and the closing of the sale is ego-enhancing. In successful salespeople, the ego drive is balanced by empathy, which is the ability to feel as the other person does. Mayer and Greenberg observed, "A salesperson simply cannot sell well without the invaluable and irreplaceable ability to get a powerful feedback from the client through empathy."

> *"Always tell the truth, not only because it is the decent thing to do but because it gives you such an advantage over the man who is trying to remember his lies!"*
> —Sam Brookes

Salespeople who have strong empathy are able to sense the feelings and reactions of their customers and adjust accordingly. "They have the drive, the need to make the sale, and their empathy gives them the connecting tool with which to do it." Our observations suggest that perhaps 20 percent of salespeople have that perfect balance of healthy ego drive and empathetic outlook.

As part of their research, Mayer and Greenberg looked at the sales aptitude tests that were commonly used to screen sales candidates at the time. They found that the tests failed for several reasons: They identified interests but not abilities, were not validated and therefore easy to manipulate, favored group conformity rather than individual creativity, and isolated fractional traits rather than revealing the dynamics of the whole person.

Fortunately, times have changed, and companies now have access to assessment tools (not merely tests) that really work.

Today's Best Practices

From the work of Marston, as well as other pioneers in the field, including Abraham Maslow (Maslow's Hierarchy of Needs), Carl Jung, Katherine Briggs and Isabel Myers (Myers-Briggs Type Indicator), David Kiersey, and Robert Hartman (Hartman Value Profile), we know today that the best way to use assessments in the

> *"Look at where your most successful people come from and go back to the same source when you're looking for new people. You may find that's a rich breeding ground for top talent."*
>
> —Richard D. Dickerson

workplace is by taking a whole person approach. A single instrument provides a limited view of a person's qualifications and may not be an accurate indicator of how people will actually perform. A whole person assessment—one that indicates behavior, skill, values, and attitudes—is what will give you the most complete picture and provide you with the information you need to make good hiring decisions.

It's important to remember that assessment tools are not tests in the traditional sense in which the individual either passes or fails. The tool may look like a test because it asks questions, but the answers are not right or wrong and the result isn't pass or fail. We may occasionally use the term

Hunters or Farmers?

Salespeople typically fall into one of two primary styles: hunters and farmers. The hunter is the transactional salesperson who is energized by the thrill of the chase and closing the deal but who just wants to move on once the sale is made. We say the hunter eats what he kills and moves on to the next target. The farmer is the service/consultant type of salesperson. The farmer plants, grows, nurtures, and harvests, and then does it all again.

The ideal for most sales cultures is to find people who can operate in both styles, but that's not easy. Most hunters won't do well in an environment more suited for farmers, and vice versa. After you benchmark your sales positions (which we'll explain in Strategy Three), you can determine which sales style is best for your culture and look for appropriate candidates.

"test" in describing the various assessment tools because it's less cumbersome, but we encourage you to avoid using "test" when discussing assessments, especially with applicants.

What Assessment Tools Should You Use?

All assessment tools are not created equal. Be sure the tools you use are validated for hiring by a traditional statistical validation process so you know you are actually measuring what you want to measure. Keep in mind that there are a number of excellent assessment tools out there that measure various personality aspects. Those tools can be used for relationship-related issues (dating compatibility, marriage and family counseling, etc.), but they are not necessarily appropriate for hiring. To repeat: Be sure the tools you use are validated for hiring. You also want to be sure the tools you use are non-discriminatory, EEOC-compliant, and meet all legal requirements. The assessment tools you use should be fair and unbiased.

So what makes a good assessment tool? If it actually measures what it claims to measure, if it does so consistently and reliably, if it is purpose-relevant, and if by using that tool, more effective decisions can be made by and about individuals, then you have a good tool. The source from which you obtain your assessment tools should be able to answer your questions and provide you with evidence as to the quality and appropriateness of the tests you are considering.

Once an individual has passed your initial screening, usually with an application or a resume that indicates the person has met your basic requirements, you can begin the assessment process. Let's take a brief look at the different types of assessments:

1. *Mental and physical ability tests*. Ability tests can be useful to identify what a candidate can do as well as to discover training needs and measure ability to learn. General ability

tests typically measure one or more broad mental abilities, such as verbal, mathematical, and reasoning skills. Specific ability tests include measures of distinct physical and mental abilities, such as reaction time, written comprehension, mathematical reasoning, and mechanical ability. Most sales positions will not require a physical ability test, although some may require a certain level of strength and endurance.

2. *Proficiency tests*. Also known as achievement tests, these tests are often used to measure current knowledge or skills in a specific area. They generally use one of two formats: a knowledge test, which includes specific questions designed to identify how much the candidate knows about a particular job; and a performance test, which requires the candidate to perform one or more of the job-related tasks.

3. *Interest inventories*. An assessment that measures interests is one of the least effective tools to use in hiring salespeople. It can tell you about a candidate's likes and dislikes, but isn't effective at predicting performance.

4. *Professional and personal values measures*. These instruments evaluate the relative importance of job activities and conditions to a candidate. Work values tests typically ask candidates to rate the importance of characteristics such as job security, income potential, or the opportunity to demonstrate creativity on the job. Personal values instruments deal with broader value structures that relate to an individual's personal as well as professional life, and they measure such issues as the importance of family, religion, and physical activity.

> "Individual characteristics are not good or bad—they simply are. It's how you manage them that matters."
>
> —JK Harris

5. *Personality assessments*. Personality inventories can

help you learn about a candidate's personal, emotional, and social traits and behaviors so you can evaluate such characteristics as motivation, conscientiousness, and self-confidence.

6. *Interviews*. Probably the most common assessment tool, interviews can be conducted in a variety of ways. For a sales

Use Assessments to Eliminate Personal Bias

It's very common for people with hiring responsibility—especially if they are not human resource professionals—to select candidates that they like or who are like them. Every interviewer will have a personal bias; it's human nature, but it's risky in the hiring process. The reason small organizations so often develop a culture that matches the owner is that the owner does all the initial hiring and he hires mirror images of himself. That's a recipe for mediocrity at best and failure at worst, especially if you have a situation such as when the owner is an operations person who is trying to hire salespeople.

It's very similar to a selling situation: People buy based on emotion from people they like and trust, and then justify their decision with logic and reason. If not otherwise trained, managers will hire people who are like themselves because we usually *like* people who are like ourselves. The problem with this approach is twofold: 1) the people you hire may not be your best candidates, and 2) you will build a team that is essentially one-dimensional.

One of the strongest arguments for using assessments is that they can minimize the influence of personal bias in the hiring process. No matter how much you like—or even dislike—a candidate, an objective, verified assessment will allow you to make a fair evaluation of whether or not that person is a good fit for the position and your organization.

position, we recommend applying the interviewing advice in Strategy One.

> *"The very best performers are first self-aware."*
> —Richard D. Dickerson

We recommend a single tool that will combine the results of the first five tools, followed by a series of interviews before you make your hiring decision. We use a tool developed by The Brooks Group and TTI called the TriMetrix which measures the how, why, will, and can questions discussed in Strategy One.

Explaining the Assessment Process to Candidates

Let each candidate know that your hiring process includes an assessment of skills, behaviors, values, and attitudes. Emphasize that this is not a test, that there are no right or wrong answers, no good or bad results. Your goal is to find the best possible fit for your culture and make sure that everyone who joins your organization has the opportunity to be successful. Stress that this is a benefit to both you and the candidate.

Communicate this both orally and in writing. You can post it on the employment opportunities page of your website and as part of any written materials you provide to candidates. During your first conversation with a candidate, explain it again. The better you are at fully explaining this part of your hiring process, the more effective it will be.

Remember that some people have a fear of taking tests, which is why it's so critical to explain that assessments are not pass/fail exams. Others may be concerned that the assessment tools will violate their privacy by revealing personal details they don't want you to know. Assure them that this is not the case.

Can a Candidate Cheat on the Assessment?

At one point or another, we have probably all said something we knew wasn't entirely accurate because we decided to say what we thought the other person wanted to hear. Certainly every man whose wife has asked, "Do I look fat in this?" can relate to this. Most of us at one time or another have done things like praise a boss's idea we didn't like rather than say what we truly thought. Can a candidate essentially do that with an assessment tool? It's possible, especially with less sophisticated tools that are not validated for hiring. For example, when Administaff, a leading professional employer organization (PEO), came to The Brooks Group for help with their sales force turnover—which was approaching a rate of 50 percent—they had been using a pre-employment assessment tool, but it wasn't effective at identifying candidates that were a fit for the company's culture. Marty Scirratt, Administaff's vice president of sales, told us: "Sales reps get tested so much that they know how to fool some tests, but [TriMetrix] provided me a way to check for inconsistencies."

When you use a quality tool that has been validated for hiring, it's extremely difficult to cheat. These tools not only provide the assessment, but they also let you know if the candidate is attempting to manipulate the results. In many cases when the assessment reveals inconsistencies such as conflicting motivators, you may want to talk to the candidate, re-explain the process, and allow the assessment to be taken again. If the assessment indicates a strong level of deception, you probably want to just pass on the candidate.

The primary area where we have found candidates attempting to cheat the assessment is when the process is handled online rather than in your office. At JK Harris & Company, for example, all candidates for every position complete the application and take the assessment online before we bring them in for an interview. We have had candidates ask someone else to take the assessment for them in the hopes of increasing their chances of being hired. The flaw in that thinking is that it's so easy for us to find out. When they come in for a face-to-face interview, or even are called for a phone interview, it is usually quickly apparent that the person we're talking to is not person who answered the assessment questions. We know what behaviors are consistent with the assessment results, so it's easy to tell, for example, if an introvert had an extrovert do the assessment for him.

When you are evaluating assessment tools, ask to see the third-party validation of the tool's accuracy and reliability. It's also a good idea to ask the company providing the tool for references from satisfied clients.

——— KEY LESSONS ———

* Two characteristics that are consistently present in high-achieving salespeople are a healthy ego drive and empathetic outlook.

* A whole person assessment that indicates behavior, skills, values, and attitudes and is validated for hiring will give you the most complete picture of candidates.

* Salespeople typically fall into one of two styles: hunters and farmers. The hunter is the transactional salesperson, and the farmer is the service/consultant salesperson.

* A good assessment tool measures what it claims to, does it consistently and reliably, is purpose-relevant, and allows more effective decisions to be made by and about people.

* The different types of assessment instruments are mental and physical ability tests, proficiency tests, interest inventories, professional and personal values measures, personality assessments, and interviews.

✳ It is very common for people with hiring responsibility to select candidates they like or who are like them. Assessments can eliminate this personal bias.

✳ Let each candidate know that your hiring process includes an assessment of their skills, behaviors, values, and attitudes. Emphasize that this is not a test and that there are no right or wrong answers and no good or bad results.

✳ It's extremely difficult to cheat an assessment when you use a quality tool that has been validated for hiring.

Define Your Target with Benchmarks

The benchmarking process is critical because it is the yardstick by which all future salespeople will be measured. This may be the most difficult and time-consuming part of reaching the Sales Flashpoint, but it is absolutely essential. You want to set a standard that is not based on the people who are currently in the job—you want the job itself to tell you what is necessary for success in your culture in terms of behaviors, values, and attitudes.

It's common for companies to decide to implement benchmarking and use their existing top performers as the benchmark. The risk in that approach is: What if your top performers aren't the best you could have? What if they are just C players when compared to other salespeople in your industry? If you base your benchmark on mediocre performers, that's all you'll ever get. If you want to build a team of A and B players, salespeople who will perform above average, you need to benchmark to the job. If you don't, you risk getting the cream of the crap rather than the cream of the crop.

When you benchmark to people, you are assuming that they are the reason for their success and that they are consistently successful. That's not necessarily true. By benchmarking to the job, you may find that the success of your top performers is due more to circumstances beyond their control than by what they are actually doing.

When you benchmark to the job, you also protect yourself on EEOC issues because you are comparing candidates to the characteristics required by the job, not the characteristics of other individuals, which could be perceived as discriminatory. This also applies to using benchmarks for training and development of your current team. This gives you an unbiased tool to show people how they compare to the needs of the job and what they can do to improve. By identifying the requirements of the job, you can compare everyone in that position to the same standard and you can ask people to commit to improvement in very specific areas. When people have committed to improving, holding them accountable is easy.

One of The Brooks Group's clients is a company in the highly competitive medical device industry. When the company began using whole person assessments in its hiring process, there was an immediate improvement in the quality of new hires. That was good, but not good enough because the company leaders really wanted to reach the Sales Flashpoint. So they agreed to benchmark the sales and sales management positions.

The conventional wisdom of the industry was that money was the most important driver for sales success. But with benchmarking, we found that money was actually second; the most important success driver was product knowledge and how the product compared with other devices. The job called for an in-depth knowledge of the company's product and the industry, as well as a willingness to build relationships with the physicians and share that knowledge. We found that the salespeople who were money-motivated

The Bonus of Benchmarking: Career Path Management

Benchmarking not only helps you hire the right person for the position, it can help everyone in your organization with career path management by letting people see a clear picture of each position so they can decide what jobs they really want to do. For example, it is very common for companies to promote top salespeople to sales managers, but that's usually a mistake (something we discuss in greater detail in Strategy Eleven). In the case of the medical device company we told you about on page 38, there is a position in the organization called a clinical specialist. The people in this position work closely with both the sales representatives and the physicians, actually standing in the operating room with the surgeons to make sure the device is properly used.

Many of the clinical specialists wanted to move into a sales position for three primary reasons: 1) It meant more money, 2) it was viewed as a promotion, and 3) it was an accepted career path in the organization. The problem was that when the company "promoted" a clinical specialist to sales representative, that person rarely achieved the same performance results as salespeople hired from other sources. The type of person who did well as a clinical specialist was not motivated by money, was not particularly competitive or concerned about winning but was very nurturing, relative, and supportive. The type of person who did well as a sales rep was competitive, sought recognition for achievements, and saw money as a measure of success.

When you benchmark positions—and we recommend you do this for every position in your company—people can clearly see what those jobs require in terms of skills, behaviors, values, and attitudes. With that information, they can make a better decision about their career paths.

were not paying sufficient attention to the physicians who were actually implanting the devices in their patients. They were transaction-oriented (hunters) when the position called for a more nurturing-oriented (farmer) type of salesperson. The salespeople who were driven more by a desire to help and to win had better relationships with the doctors and enjoyed high economic rewards as a result—but they weren't driven by the money. The top performers turned out to not be as good as had been thought because they weren't really the best fit for the job. Once the company benchmarked and began hiring to the benchmark, rather than attempting to match the characteristics of previously successful salespeople, sales began to soar.

Benchmarking Steps

Benchmarking provides clarity and awareness about the job and eliminates bias in the hiring process by letting the job tell you what it needs in terms of personal and professional skills, attitudes and values.

Here's how to do it.

Listen to the Job

Consider how you are currently doing the job and how the job should be done—chances are, those two things are not a perfect match. Benchmark on how the job *should* be done. Think in terms of what would happen in an ideal world, if there were no excuses and no exceptions. Don't think about human characteristics; focus on the job and what it requires. You want the cleanest, least-biased picture of what the job looks like—*not* a profile of the people currently in the job.

If the job could talk, what would it say about itself? To find out, gather a group of stakeholders and subject matter experts and ask them.

Who Participates?

The people who should be involved in the benchmarking process are both stakeholders—that is, people with a vested interest in seeing this job performed well—and subject matter experts, those who are very familiar with the requirements of the job. This group can include people who currently do the job and are performing well, have done the job, understand the job, manage the job, created the job, interface with the job, or are in some way close to the job. Carefully screen the participants who will be involved in this process. It's important that the people involved in benchmarking any given job truly understand the job. And as obvious as that sounds, we have seen situations where, for example, a company owner has brought a friend or relative into the organization at a senior level, and that person is simply not fit for this particular process, but the owner insists that he be involved. Though a good benchmarking program can remove the impact of bias (or ignorance, as the case may be), it's still better to choose the participants with sufficient care so that inaccurate or extreme perceptions do not cause the final benchmark to be skewed.

> *"It's kind of fun to do the impossible."*
> —Walt Disney

Depending on the size of your organization and the complexity of the job, you should have between three and 10 stakeholders and subject matter experts to develop an effective benchmark.

The Benchmarking Process

Begin with a meeting or conference call involving all the stakeholders you've identified to explain what you're doing and get everybody on the same page. That's not as simple as it sounds. We have found in the pre-benchmarking meeting or call that there is an amazing amount of confusion, disagreement, and different perceptions of jobs. Don't assume that everyone in your organization views any given job in the same way; in fact, it's highly unlikely that is the case. What is far more common is a significant lack of consistency in how jobs are viewed. You need to get that out on the table so you can begin listening to the job itself rather than people's perceptions—and get the people who are stakeholders in the process to examine their perceptions for accuracy.

The next step is to get that group of stakeholders to answer questions and rank statements about the job. Every stakeholder should answer the same set of questions so any conflicts in perceptions of the job can be addressed. The stakeholders also need to respond honestly based on their perceptions of the job, not on what they think someone else wants to hear. You may be surprised at the difference between how you see a particular job and how your employees see it. How a job can be viewed so differently by different people can be quite eye-opening for a company's leadership.

The questions and statements should relate to the various tasks or characteristics that would be prevalent in the job. For example, one of the statements may be: "Ability to handle stress is important for success in this job" and the stakeholder is asked to pick one response: "very important," "important," "not important," or "not applicable." Keep in mind that not more than 30 percent of the questions should qualify to be answered as "very important"—if all the tasks and characteristics were "very important," no human being would ever be able to do that job.

"The only place success comes before work is in the dictionary."
—Vince Lombardi

After the questions are answered, the responses should be compiled, and a follow-up meeting or conference call held to discuss the results and make sure that the benchmark truly reflects the perceptions of all the participants. Be sure there is complete agreement. If any of the stakeholders disagree, look at that issue and make the necessary and appropriate changes until you reach a unanimous decision.

It's possible to develop your own questionnaire to use for benchmarking, but it is far more effective and efficient to use a professionally designed program, such as the one developed by The Brooks Group and TTI that is scientifically designed to minimize the impact of personal bias. It's also a good idea to use an outsider to facilitate the process because that person is objective without any experience-related biases.

Before you begin, explain to every participant how critical this process is and the huge impact it will have on the company. Let everyone who will be part of the exercise know what will be required of them and send complete instructions in advance. Remember you will be defining forevermore what this job looks like in your culture and how every candidate going forward will be evaluated. Certainly at any point in the future you could change the benchmark, and there may be valid reasons, such as a buyout or a cultural shift. Even so, don't let the fact that you can change a benchmark be an excuse to be sloppy about the process.

Define and Justify the Job

Once the stakeholders have reached an agreement of what the job looks like, update the current job description, if there is one. If there isn't, you have the information you need to create one. Use feedback and gain consensus from the subject matter experts as you do this. It's critical to develop a clear and detailed answer to the question: Why does this job exist?

View the position from four angles:

1. The actual position and what it takes to perform the work

2. How the position relates to the final customer

3. How the position impacts the bottom line

4. Changes that may occur in the industry or job that the position will need to keep up-to-date with

Define the key accountabilities of the job. A key accountability is a concise statement that defines a specific group of tasks the job requires for superior performance. Focus on the big picture, not the tasks, but incorporate enough detail for a clear definition. For example, it's not enough to say that a sales job requires that the person sell the company's products and it's too much to say that the job requires that customer phone calls be returned the same day.

Once you have defined the key accountabilities, prioritize them in order of importance to the job, not according to the amount of time spent doing them. The most important key accountability may not take the most time. For example, if your salespeople are responsible for doing their own prospecting (and

Benchmark Minimums

To be effective, every benchmark should answer the following questions:

- What is the purpose and objective of this position?

- How does this position affect the delivery of the product or service to the customer?

- How does staying abreast of industry- or job-related knowledge impact the success of this position?

- How does the effectiveness and efficiency of this position affect the company's bottom line?

not all salespeople are), that's a key accountability that is extremely important, but it's probably not what you want a salesperson to spend most of his time doing.

> "Sometimes you have to do things that are painful in the short term to strengthen and grow your business for the long term."
> —JK Harris

When you have defined and prioritized the key accountabilities, assign a percentage of the week each will be focused on. Only assign 80 percent of the workweek so that you allow time for the unexpected.

Though we are focusing on sales positions, it's worth noting that if you do this process for every position in your company, you may identify some jobs that you don't need and can eliminate, or that can be combined with other positions or adjusted in other ways to be more productive and cost-efficient.

Compare Candidates and Current Employees to the Benchmark

When you have done a whole person assessment on your candidates so you know who you are hiring and a thorough benchmark on the job, it's easy to compare the candidates to the benchmark and identify the ones with potential for success in the position.

It's important to recognize that using a whole person assessment and benchmarking does not provide a 100 percent guarantee of success—even though our experience has shown that the success rate for companies that do this is extremely high. What it does tell you is that all indications are that the individual you have hired has the skills, attitudes, and behaviors necessary for success in your organization.

Historically and with the exception of some sort of catastrophic circumstances, when someone didn't perform as expected, it was due to one (or a combination) of three reasons: a bad hire, poor training, or poor management. And we'll be addressing those issues in later strategies. When you use a whole person assessment and benchmarking, you narrow down the reason someone doesn't perform as expected to two possibilities: poor training or poor management.

It's also a good idea to compare your current employees to the benchmark to see if they are where they need to be. Some companies decide to grandfather in their current employees, leaving them where they are even though they're not a good fit, but that's not the best approach. Comparing current employees to the benchmark for their positions could reveal the need for some staffing changes. Take a look at these people and how they fit. No one should be sacrosanct. You may have some people whose performance could improve with coaching. You may identify others who could be moved into other positions. And, painful though it might be, you may identify people who need to be let go.

There has never been a better time to implement whole person assessments and benchmarking tools. It's easy to get into a hiring rut when things are going well because you can afford mediocrity. In good times, everybody is a good candidate. But in bad times, you need to be able to differentiate the good from the bad and hire the best people for your positions and culture. If your company downsized during the economic recession of 2008–09, you have a tremendous opportunity to do things right as the recovery gets underway.

——— KEY LESSONS ———

※ The benchmark for your sales positions is the yardstick by which all future salespeople will be measured.

※ A benchmark lets the job itself tell you what is necessary for success in your culture in terms of behaviors, values, and attitudes.

* Benchmark the job, not the people who are doing it. That gives you an accurate picture of the best person to fill the job.

* Benchmark every position in your company. This not only helps you hire the right person for each position, but it helps everyone in your organization with career path management.

* Benchmark on how the job *should* be done, not how you are currently doing it.

* The people involved in the benchmarking process should be stakeholders, who are those with a vested interest in seeing the job performed well, and subject matter experts, who are familiar with the requirements of the job.

* Begin with a meeting or conference with all the stakeholders and subject matter experts to explain what you're doing. Get them to answer questions and rank statements about the job. Compile those responses and go back to the group for further discussion until you have complete agreement.

* View each job from four angles: the actual position and what it takes to perform the work, how the position relates to the final customer, how the position impacts the bottom line, and changes that may occur that could affect the position.

* Define key accountabilities and prioritize them in order of importance to the job, not according to the amount of time spent doing them.

* Every benchmark should include the purpose and objective of the position, how the position affects delivery of the product or service to the customer, how staying abreast of industry- or job-related knowledge impacts the success of the position, and how the effectiveness and efficiency of the position affects the company's bottom line.

✳ Compare candidates to the benchmark to identify the ones with potential for success in the position.

✳ Compare current employees to the benchmark to see if they are where they need to be and make changes if necessary.

part two

Train Right

No one is so good at what they do that they can't benefit from training. There's always something new to learn, a new strategy to try. If you're going to get the best performance from your sales team, you need to provide them with the best information and techniques when you train them—material that is up to date and relevant to the real world. We call it keeping the ax sharpened.

Top performing salespeople are very systematic in their approach. We recommend that you train your sales team to use a system. The next seven strategies are based on a proven sales system known as IMPACT, which was developed by The Brooks Group.

Build Sales with IMPACT

Once you have the right people on board, the next step is to train them on a comprehensive sales system that will allow them to achieve consistent results. Research conducted by The Brooks Group has shown that when a salesperson follows a linked, sequential selling process that is customer-focused and principles-based, his chance of completing the sale is 93 percent. Without such a system, the chance falls to 42 percent.

The research involved interviewing approximately 8,500 CEOs and, with their permission, video-recording them being called upon by salespeople. The CEOs were not specifically asked to evaluate whether or not the salespeople used a system, but they recognized that the salespeople who did use a system were better than the ones who didn't. In particular, they said that when the salesperson used a sequential process, especially one that allowed the customers to make decisions at their own pace, they were more likely to buy. The research showed that which system the salesperson was using did not seem to matter as much as the fact that the salesperson was using a system and not just winging it. Salespeople who use a customer-focused system are perceived as better prepared and more professional and focused on the buyer as an individual than on completing a sale and making a commission. Customers are more likely to believe that those salespeople genuinely have their best interests at heart and, consequently, they are more likely to buy.

The system that we recommend is IMPACT. It was developed by The Brooks Group and, when coupled with a selection process that includes a whole person assessment, produces a team of sales superstars. The following six strategies will examine each element of the IMPACT system in more detail, but one of the most important things we want to stress about this system is:

The secret to selling is to be in front of qualified prospects when they are ready to buy, not when you need to make a sale.

A strong sales system will include sufficient emphasis on preparation so your salespeople know how to find and qualify prospects. They won't waste time making presentations to prospects who are not qualified and ready to buy. Even better, because they use a proven system, they will close sales often enough that they won't get desperate and have their own need to make a sale color their presentations.

What we're talking about here is how well your salespeople are positioned. If they are relying on cold calling as a way to make sales, they are positioning themselves as more self-focused and less customer-focused. They are using a technique that is generally not well-received. While cold calling may be appropriate for certain types of products or industries, it is not the approach of choice for today's top performing salespeople. Cold calling says you don't really care anything about your customer because you are willing to interrupt them and make a sales pitch when you know nothing about their

needs and wants; it says all you care about is making a sale. Customers don't care whether or not you need to make a sale; they care about what they want and need. The best salespeople understand that it isn't about them—it's all about their prospect or customer.

We should point out that while cold calling is not an effective sales method, it can be a good prospecting tool. We are not saying that you should

> "One out of two college graduates will end up in a sales or sales-related job, but most of them have no training in sales. If you want them to excel, you must give them the tools they need."
>
> —Richard D. Dickerson

never cold call; we are saying that you should use cold calls in the way that they will yield the best results.

Another fatal flaw we see in mediocre or low-performing salespeople is that they get so focused on what they want to happen that they lose sight of what the *prospect* wants to happen. Certainly salespeople need to recognize what they want—which is generally going to be to complete the sale, earn a commission, build a new relationship, and create potential for future business—but they need to focus on what the customers want as well, which is to buy on their own terms. Successful salespeople are willing to find a way to understand and provide what their customers want. When they focus on that, rather than on what they want, the sales process goes far more smoothly and produces results that work for everyone.

What is IMPACT?

IMPACT is the sales system developed and taught by The Brooks Group. The term is an acronym that stands for the six steps in the process:

1. Investigate
2. Meet
3. Probe
4. Apply

5. Convince

6. Tie it up

Keys to Making Any Sales System Work

1. Don't skip any of the steps.

2. Don't leave a step until you have completed it.

3. Make sure you and your prospect are in the same step at the same time.

Rules of the IMPACT Selling System

The rules of the IMPACT selling system are very simple:

1. *Never skip a step.* Follow the system in the order it was developed. There is research and logic behind the process that has been proved to work, and skipping steps or changing the order will likely have a negative impact on the results.

2. *Don't leave a step until you've completed it.* This prevents both the salesperson and the prospect from going too fast and missing important details.

3. *Make sure you and your prospect are on the same step.* You will know by the prospect's responses whether or not you are on the same step. If you get out of sync, it's the salesperson's responsibility to recognize it and circle back.

Are there times when you can break one or more of these rules and still make the sale? Yes, but they're rare. For example, if a prospect says at the very beginning, "I'm familiar with your company and your product, and I'd like to buy it," you can forego finding out what the prospect wants and proving that your product can satisfy those wants. But most of the time, you should go through each step because even when you feel you don't have to, your prospect does. And prospects usually won't buy until they have been through all the steps themselves and are comfortable with their decision.

An invisible barrier exists between every buyer and seller—a barrier of feelings that range from apathy to resistance. Most people are going to be at least a little uneasy with salespeople. Whether it's through personal experience, the experience of others, or the media, some people have learned to view sales professionals at least somewhat adversarially or with a degree of distrust. That creates a barrier of resistance. Others see salespeople as peddlers not worth caring about, and that creates a barrier of apathy.

Salespeople need to find a way to penetrate the barrier to gain the attention and eventual respect of each prospect. Using a sequentially linked process that is customer-focused will allow your sales team to do that.

When you combine a proven sales system with salespeople chosen by a validated whole person assessment tool as described in Strategy Two, you can feed those individual behavioral, attitudinal, and selling skills into each step of the sales system for maximum results. Salespeople who have gone through the whole person assessment and understand their own strengths and challenges will, with the help of a strong manager, be able to figure out what they need to do and to change to perform better in each step. For example, do they need to modify their style to be more assertive and comfortable when meeting a prospect? Do they appear to be too cool and distant, and if so, would they be more successful if they could be more open? Do they naturally tend to talk a lot (many extroverts do), and do they need to make a conscious effort to talk less and listen more?

Blending the system with the whole person assessment lets you go beyond investing in skill development, as important as that is. It lets you refine attitudes, which in turn enhances the use of your skills.

Who Are Your Most Qualified Prospects?

> "We are what we repeatedly do. Excellence, then, is not an act, but a habit."
> —Aristotle

Your salespeople need to be investing their time and energies not just with qualified prospects but with the *most* qualified prospects. All prospects are not created equal! Some are more qualified than others and the better job your salespeople do at finding and attracting qualified prospects, the more successful they will be. That's why the salespeople on your team need to be focusing their attention on prospects with these characteristics:

1. Awareness that they have a need and a reasonably clear understanding of what that need is.
2. Authority to buy and ability to pay.
3. A sense of urgency.
4. A receptiveness to developing trust and rapport.
5. A willingness to listen.

> "Everyone lives by selling something."
> —Robert Louis Stevenson

When you find a prospect with all five characteristics, you've hit the jackpot. But even if a prospect has just a few, or even just one of these, you're in a better position than if they have none.

What Do Your Prospects Really Want?

As with just about everything, customers have evolved over the years. It used to be that they just wanted your product or service, and the salesperson didn't matter too much. Then we went through a period when customers wanted to develop a relationship with both the salesperson and the company, which is how relationship selling came to be.

Today, what prospects really want and demand of providers and salespeople is a solution to their issues and problems—a solution to

the things that are keeping them up at night. That may involve a relationship, or it may not. It may involve different kinds of relationships, products, and services. It's up to you to figure that out and present the solution to your prospects.

> *"Show people what they want most, and they will move heaven and earth to get it."*
> —Frank Bettger

The Difference Between Needs and Wants

Many sales systems are obsessed with meeting the prospect's needs. This is not bad as far as it goes, but it's not enough. What's more important is that you identify and fulfill your prospect's *wants*.

Let's look at the difference between needs and wants. Needs are typically product-specific and fact-oriented. They are rational and easy to define and articulate. By contrast, wants are usually unrelated

Concentrate on Your Niche

Your niche is that place in the market where you are best known or where you have a competitive advantage. Start and spend most of your time in your niche, whether it's transportation, health care, manufacturing or whatever.

It's a good idea to identify segments within your niche to further target your sales efforts. For example, the transportation niche would include segments such as passenger, heavy freight, small package shipping, document shipping, ocean freight, international and so on. Segments in the health-care niche could include hospitals, physicians' offices, rehab centers, assisted living centers and so on.

When you try to sell outside your niche, it's almost a guarantee that you'll run up against overwhelming obstacles that you are not prepared to deal with. It doesn't make sense to do that to yourself and your company. Find and focus on your niche and the rest will fall into place.

to a specific product and are emotion-based and perception-oriented. When it comes to wants, what matters is not the reality but what the prospect perceives the reality to be.

Consider your own buying habits. You often buy what you need; you *always* buy what you want. For example, you need to eat, and a hamburger will meet that need. Sometimes you want the hamburger, but other times you want a medium-rare filet mignon. You need clothes, but you might want the ones with the designer label. You need transportation, but the make and model of car you buy will depend on what you want.

All buying—whether it's consumers buying for themselves or a purchasing agent buying for a company—is driven by emotions. People make their buying decisions based on emotion (and what they want), then look for logic and reason to justify those decisions. Top salespeople understand why people buy and how they reach their buying decisions, and they have developed their ability to persuade—not manipulate—people to make a decision in their favor. Remember, people can usually sense when they're being manipulated; they don't like it and they will resist it. Manipulation is defined as exerting shrewd or devious influence, especially for one's own advantage. It's not the way to achieve long-term sales success. Persuasion, by contrast, is a communication intended to induce belief or action. When you manipulate, you try to get people to do what you want them to do, regardless of what they want or need. When you persuade, you are showing people why doing business with you is to their best advantage so that they will make that choice because *they* want to, not because you tricked them. Basic persuasion techniques include reciprocation, commitment and consistency, social proof, liking, authority, and scarcity.

Reciprocation is based on the fact that when you do something for someone else, you create a feeling of indebtedness. This is why giving product samples is such an effective sales technique: You give a prospect a free sample (gift) and he will feel that he must reciprocate in some way, and that way is usually by purchasing.

This is not to suggest that you should "buy" business by giving customers gifts, and we recognize that it isn't practical to offer samples for every product or service. But you should understand the psychology behind this technique. It's why we offer the *Flashpoints* newsletter for free (visit theflashpoints.com to subscribe)—we genuinely want you to have the information at no charge, but we also hope you will reciprocate by giving us a chance to compete for your business if you need the type of consulting services we provide.

The next persuasion technique—commitment and consistency—is based on the fact that when someone makes a personal commitment, he feels a tremendous amount of pressure to be consistent with it. This is part of the logic behind the process taught in the IMPACT system of asking feedback questions—not only do you clarify the prospect's reaction to you and your product, you are also leading him through a series of commitment statements that will ultimately result in a purchase.

Social proof uses the behavior of others to justify or prove the validity of a decision. Yes, there are a few people who genuinely want to be different, who are willing to be first with something, who are true individualists, but most of us take comfort in the approval of our peer group or in the knowledge that other people have made the same decision we have with positive results. We talk more about this in Strategy Nine.

Liking is an important part of the persuasion process because people will do things for people they like that they won't do for people they don't like. The absolute best example of this is businesses that sell through home parties. The host or hostess usually agrees to give the party because a friend—someone they like—asked them to. Most of the guests come because they like the host, not because they want to buy storage containers, jewelry, or candles. Liking plays a more subtle role in business-to-business sales relationships, but it's still important. When liking exists, the other persuasion techniques can be easily used.

The persuasion technique of authority is based on the fact that it is human nature to respond with obedience to people we view in positions of authority, such as doctors, police officers, military officers, judges, teachers, and even very well-dressed businesspeople. Top performing salespeople know how to position themselves and their companies as authorities. We talk more about that in Strategy Six.

Finally, opportunities seem more valuable to us when their availability is limited. In sales and marketing, we are using the persuasion technique of scarcity when we limit quantities (as in, "only five to a customer," or "only three in each store") or set deadlines (as in, "offer good for three days only"). But for scarcity to be effective, it must be believable. Don't claim quantities are limited if they're not. Don't set a deadline, then ignore it or change it.

When you understand persuasion, it becomes clear that what salespeople should be focusing on are *wants*, not needs. Without a doubt, needs are important. Your products or services are likely very needs-specific, and you should understand how your products' features match with your prospects' needs. But simply meeting needs is not enough. People want their needs taken care of in a way that also satisfies their wants.

What it all comes down to is this: People buy what they need from people who understand what they want. When salespeople consistently focus on the wants and needs of their prospects and customers, they consistently excel.

Focus Where it Counts

When sales teams are ranked by performance, our research has found that salespeople who are focused merely on survival and meeting quota will rank in the bottom 20 percent. The salespeople who focus on presenting the product, making money, or their own ego will rank in the middle 60 percent. But the salespeople who focus on the customers' needs and wants rank in the top 20 percent.

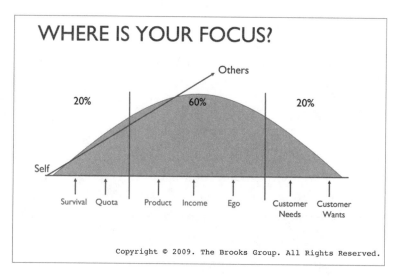

WHERE IS YOUR FOCUS?

Copyright © 2009. The Brooks Group. All Rights Reserved.

The more the salespeople shift their focus from themselves to others, the higher their performance will be.

Now let's take a look at the system that can help your sales team be the people who understand what your prospects and customers want. These are the fundamentals you need to teach each sales rep in your company. In previous strategies, we spoke more to the entrepreneur, business owner, or sales manager; for the next six strategies, we will speak directly to the salesperson and explain what they need to do to achieve rapid-fire sales growth.

——— **KEY LESSONS** ———

✳ When a salesperson follows a linked, sequential selling process that is customer-focused and principles-based, his chance of completing the sale is 93 percent. Without such a system, the chance falls to 42 percent.

✳ When salespeople rely on cold calling as a way to make sales, they are positioning themselves as self-focused rather than customer-focused.

* The keys to making any sales system work are don't skip any of the steps, don't leave a step until you have completed it, and make sure you and your prospect are in the same step at the same time.

* All prospects are not created equal. Salespeople should be investing their time and energy with the most qualified prospects.

* Qualified prospects are aware they have a need, have a reasonably clear understanding of what that need is, have the authority to buy and ability to pay, feel a sense of urgency about the purchase, are receptive to developing trust and rapport with the salesperson, and are willing to listen.

* Successful salespeople understand and focus on their niche, which is the place in the market where they are best known and have a competitive advantage.

* Needs are typically product-specific and fact-oriented; wants are emotion-based and perception-oriented.

* Persuasion is a communication intended to induce belief or action. Basic persuasion techniques include reciprocation, commitment and consistency, social proof, liking, authority, and scarcity.

* All buying is driven by emotions. People make their decisions based on emotion, which is what they want, and then look for logic and reason to justify those decisions. People buy what they need from people who understand what they want.

* Salespeople who focus on the customers' needs and wants consistently rank in the top 20 percent of sales performers. The more salespeople shift their focus from themselves to others, the higher their performance will be.

Prepare, Prepare, Prepare

The first step in the IMPACT sales system is *investigate*. That means gathering sufficient information about your market and prospects so that you are able to make the best possible sales presentation. It's the process of getting ready to sell well. It's preparation. It's research. It's all the things you can do to position yourself as the best qualified person to talk to, the true expert your customers need to deliver what they want.

Positioning and Branding

Positioning is how you and your organization are seen in the marketplace. It's what prospects and customers think of when they hear your name and your organization's name. Branding is related to

positioning and is the emotional side of how you, your company, and your products are perceived in the market.

It takes a lot of work and time to develop a strong brand because successful brands are built on many, many acts of integrity and development. A brand starts with a name, logo, and slogan, but it's built on a promise. Consistently delivering on that promise is what builds a brand. People come to trust it; they see the brand more as an experience than a product. And here's something interesting about companies with strong brands: Very often, they have the weakest sales force. The brand tends to carry the company and the salespeople tend to hide behind the brand. Companies with leaders who are savvy enough to build strong brands *and* strong sales teams have an unbeatable advantage when it comes to growth and profits.

Another interesting fact about positioning and branding is that your own personal positioning, how you as an individual are viewed in the marketplace, can supersede your organization's positioning, its products or services, and even its brands. This is because people still buy from people. People form relationships with people, not brands. People look to people, not things, for solutions.

Consider how you want to be perceived by your customers. Be seen as someone with whom time would be well-spent. Part of your personal foundation as a successful salesperson is to take the necessary steps to position yourself as an expert, trusted advisor, and ally to your customers. Strong positioning is achieved with thorough preparation. In fact, be over-prepared. Close to 90 percent of today's buyers have already researched what they want on the internet, and they often know more about it than the salespeople calling on them. They know the pricing,

> "Chance is always powerful.
> Let your hook be always cast.
> In the pool where you least
> expect it will be a fish."
>
> —Ovid

markup, features, guarantees, availability, supplier's reputation and more. So don't go in expecting to be perceived as an authority unless you truly are. Don't go in claiming to know everything unless you really do because you're likely to get zinged with a question you can't answer. Do your homework. Know what information is out there and available about your product or service and be able to cite your sources.

The more successful you are at positioning yourself as an expert, the more successful you will be in sales because to

Cold Calling or Warm Calling?

The late Peter Drucker analyzed cold-calling results over a range of U.S. industries. He found that you have a 1 in 14 chance of being successful on a cold call. That means you have to make 14 calls to get just one yes—or even one maybe. That's not a particularly appealing strategy, is it? And the ratio in your business may be different. It could be less, but it could be 1 in 200 or even 1 in 500. As a sales strategy, cold calling is probably the least effective thing you can do. It pays to spend your time carefully planning your activities and qualifying prospects—not just randomly knocking on doors. Too often, salespeople just run out blindly and call on anybody. They don't take the time to qualify the prospect so that they know if it's even necessary or worthwhile to go see them. Always call on your most qualified prospects first. Spend your time and energy on the prospects who are most likely to buy from you.

Drucker also discovered that you have a 1 in 4 chance of being successful when you're calling on someone you used to do business with and stopped for some reason. You have a 1 in 2 chance of doing more business with an existing customer, which proves what most salespeople know well: The best source of new business is an existing customer. Always look to your current customers for either an opportunity to increase their business with you or as referral sources.

> *"The expectations of life depend upon diligence; the mechanic that would perfect his work must first sharpen his tools."*
>
> —Confucius

prospects and customers, the salesperson *is* the product, service, or organization. In many cases when you call on prospects, they don't know anybody else in your company except you—which means you *are* the company to them. Their impression of you will be their impression of your organization, so make it a good one.

Common Positioning Mistakes

Let's take a look at some of the common mistakes salespeople—especially new ones—make when it comes to positioning.

- *Relying too much on cold calling.* This typically happens because the sales manager has told them to get out of the office and go do something—to get their "feet on the street." So they start roaming around, cold calling. But think about this: Someone just walks into your office, interrupts your day, wants to take up your valuable time telling you about something you probably have no desire for—and even if you did, you'd want to buy it on your own terms. How likely would you be to buy from that person?

  When used as a sales strategy, cold calls are a sign that someone is self-focused and desperate. Cold calling is more than unprofessional; it's a very inefficient, ineffective use of your time. The exception to this is when cold calling is used as a prospecting strategy, but even then, you must be careful to avoid positioning yourself as someone who is desperate. There are plenty of other ways to prospect, which we'll discuss shortly.

- *Being too pushy or being too much of a pest.* Sometimes the difference between being annoyingly pushy and respectably persistent is one of perception. You are a pest when people tell you that you are. You'll come across as pushy when you are focused on what you want (a sale) rather than what the prospect wants. This positions you as a nuisance, not as a respected source.

· *Appearing desperate to make a sale.* This goes with cold calling and being pushy. People are generally uncomfortable with buying from a desperate salesperson. Even if they have some interest in what's being sold, the atmosphere of desperation makes them wonder what's wrong with the salesperson, the company, or the product. Some salespeople use "I really need this sale" as a strategy; it might work under rare circumstances, but we don't recommend it, and it's not a route to consistent success.

· *Presenting yourself as the stereotypical, fast-talking salesperson.* We find it amazing, but there are some salespeople who still think the carpetbagger approach works—and, as with desperation, it might on occasion, but usually only if your audience is gullible and your product not quite on the up-and-up. The manipulative, slick talkers are focused on themselves, not on their customers, and that rarely leads to a mutually beneficial result.

· *Immediately dropping the price.* Anyone who uses price as a selling strategy is in trouble from day one. No matter what you sell and what you charge, there is always someone who will do it for less. There will always be someone who will undercut you, so don't go there. Salespeople who cut prices, and companies that support that approach, find themselves in a battle of who has the deepest pockets, who can afford to keep reducing their profit margins and possibly even operating at a loss. Yes, there are times when it makes sense to drop prices, such as when you're trying to move inventory that isn't selling or when you make a deliberate decision to

use price as a short-term competitive strategy (explained in Strategy Six, "Respect the Competition," of *Flashpoint: Seven Core Strategies for Rapid-Fire Business Growth* by JK Harris). But if your first response to a price objection is to reduce the price, you've made a serious positioning mistake.

· *Being a product-pusher.* People don't buy products; they buy solutions. Focusing on your product without presenting how it can deliver solutions will seldom end in a sale.

Four Key People You Need to Identify

During the investigate step with any new prospect, there are four key roles you need to identify:

· *Internal advocate.* This is an ally inside of an account who is clearly on your side. Your internal advocate keeps your name in front of the decision-maker and essentially sells you in your absence. This will often be the person who contacted you in the beginning or the first person you made contact with. If you're fortunate, you'll have more than one internal advocate.

· *Check writer.* This is the person who actually pays for your product, typically the controller or a senior financial person.

· *Decision maker.* This is the person who, in the final analysis, says yes or no. Most of the time, the decision maker will be one individual, but on occasion, it will be a group of people.

· *User.* The user is the person who will actually use the product or solution.

> *"There are moments when everything goes well. Don't be frightened; it won't last."*
> —Jules Renard

Sometimes each of these roles will be played by different people; sometimes the same person will play two or more roles; and sometimes there may be more than one person in a particular

The Power of a Strong Direct Value Statement

Your direct value statement, also known as an elevator speech, is a 30-second infomercial that tells people just enough about what you do in such a manner that they will respond with, "That's interesting. Tell me more." Use a direct value statement to leave a confident, effective voice message, to introduce yourself, or to get to the point of a face-to-face meeting quickly and successfully. It needs to be clear, concise, and customer-focused. It should position you as someone with whom time would be well-spent so a prospect will see immense value in talking with you further. Write it down and practice it until it sounds completely natural.

When you're trying to get an appointment with a prospect, the thing at the top of your mind is figuring out what you need to say to get that person to agree to see you. You need to also be thinking about what's going through your prospect's mind—which is likely that he's wondering who you are, who you represent, and what's in it for him if he agrees to see you. You can answer those questions with a powerful direct value statement.

As you develop your direct value statement, test it out on colleagues who will give you their honest opinion about its effectiveness, then adjust and polish it until you get the most effective phrasing possible. Note that we said test it on colleagues who will give you their honest opinion—you can't count on your mother or your spouse to give you the kind of evaluation you need because they probably think everything you say or do is wonderful, and they don't know how your customers are likely to respond. Once you get the statement polished, memorize it and use it at networking events, professional association meetings, and other situations where it would be appropriate to answer the question: "What do you do?"

role. For example, it's common for the internal advocate and the user to be the same person, especially if you're selling something

How Desperation Killed a Sale

At JK Harris & Company, documents are a huge part of the process in the services we provide to our clients, and we used to make a lot of photocopies. A couple of years ago, I (JK Harris) got a call from a woman I'll call Sandra (not her real name) who had been one of my very first clients when I opened my CPA firm. She said she was now in the copier/fax machine business and wanted to come talk to me. We scheduled an appointment, during which she persuaded me to let her do a study on our copy usage. She found that the company we had been using for several years was over-billing us by about $60,000 a year. So I gave her company the contract.

Then last year we decided we could further reduce our paper copies, document storage, and expenses with technology. I called Sandra and asked her to find three consultants to do an analysis on our operation and make recommendations for going paperless. Each consultant had a different approach, and Sandra chose the one she said she thought was best for us. I trusted her from what she had done for us in the past, but she was really putting the pressure on us to do the deal. My antenna went up, and I decided to have my own team do some further research. We discovered we could acquire the necessary software and implement the solution on our own for less than half of what the lowest-priced consultant that Sandra was pushing was asking. Now, I knew that the consultants had a commission for Sandra built into their fees and I was okay with that because she had earned it by finding them for me. But even with that in mind, they all still wanted to charge us significantly more than was necessary.

Had Sandra not been so pushy and desperate to close the deal, had she let it move along naturally, we probably would have accepted her recommendation. But her desperation caused me to do more research and cost her, and the consultant she was working with, the business.

the user really wants. Sometimes the internal advocate is the person who was assigned the task of doing the research to come up with a solution for the company's problem. In most cases, though, the internal advocate can make or break the deal, so it's important that you identify that person and nurture the relationship.

How To Position Yourself as an Industry Expert

People like to buy from experts, which is why top sales professionals invest substantial time and energy in positioning themselves as experts in their field. They don't come across as know-it-alls, but they convey knowledge and expertise in a confident manner. This enhances trust and rapport, allowing the customer to feel good about his buying decision. Here's how you can achieve a position as an expert in the eyes of your prospects and customers:

- *Research the organizations your customers belong to and join them as associate or vendor members.* Don't just pay dues; attend meetings and participate in other appropriate ways. This helps you learn about the issues that are of concern to your customers and regularly puts you in front of them and prospects in a nonsales environment. Use these opportunities wisely. Don't try to sell at meetings; use those occasions to learn and build your network. And even when the organization holds a social event, don't relax too much—you may not be on a sales call at the group's annual picnic or holiday party, but you're still there in a professional capacity and you want to maintain your image as a trustworthy expert. Inappropriate conduct can cost you a degree of respect that you will find it difficult, if not impossible, to recover.
- *Read the same journals, trade publications and other informative materials that your customers read.* You need to know what they know and understand what they understand. Be able

to make references to these sources so it's clear you are making an investment in your own expertise so that you can be of greater value to your customers.

· *Search the internet for industry information and trends. You'll find breaking news and greater detail online.* One of the easiest ways to do this is to use Google Alerts, which is a free service that will send you an e-mail when Google's search engine finds new entries for the terms you want to track. You can track industry terms, company and individual names, or other key words and phrases.

· *Ethically and professionally gather as much information as you can about your competitors and how they do business.* Ask people in your own organization—not necessarily on the sales team—who may know about these companies to give you information. Listen to what your customers have to say about them. Talk to salespeople from other companies who may have called on your competitors. Study your competitors' marketing materials; the internet makes it easier than ever to do this because it's virtually all online. If possible, secret shop your competitors so you know what sort of experience your own customers are likely to have.

· *Ask other salespeople inside and outside your organization for insight on industry trends, common customer questions, ideas for serving customers better and so on.* Find out what issues are coming up on their calls and how they're dealing with them. And, of course, be willing to share your own knowledge and experiences.

· *Dress one notch above your prospect or customer.* This gives you the visual appearance of a solution-based expert who knows the importance of respect and image. So if your prospect wears a tie, you should wear a tie and a coat (if you're a man) or a comparable suit (if you're a woman). If the prospect

Prospects Will Judge a Book by Its Cover

People judge people by how they look. Right or wrong, that's the way things are. And that's why we advise that the best general strategy is to dress just one notch above your prospects. But sometimes, one notch above is too high. That's why you need to be familiar with the customs of your industry and geographic area.

If you know nothing else about coal mining, you probably know that physically it is a dirty, ugly business. It's better now than it used to be, but even with modern technology, it's still coal mining, and coal still has to be dug out of the ground. One of my (Richard Dickerson) clients worked for a company that manufactured a particular piece of equipment used by coal mines that was very expensive—it started at $1.5 million per unit. When he first called on a coal mine in West Virginia that had annual worldwide sales exceeding $100 million, he couldn't get in to see the decision-maker. He would drive to the mine in his car, which was nice and well-maintained but not a luxury car. He never wore a tie, but he did wear nice slacks, a shirt and a blazer.

I used to work a sales territory that included West Virginia, and I learned that the people there—especially those in the coal mining industry—are hardworking folks who aren't inclined to put on airs, and they dress for the business they're in, which means they wear jeans, work shoes, and sturdy shirts. They tend to be suspicious of people who look like they don't belong, and my client looked like he didn't belong. So he bought a pickup truck and began dressing the same way his prospects dressed. He didn't look like an outsider anymore. The manager of the mine finally warmed up to him, and he was eventually able to make a sale.

It's all about trust. It's human nature to be distrustful of people who are different than we are. If you know and follow the customs of your industry, you can avoid building a barrier based on image.

doesn't wear a tie, you don't either—but leave your coat on. Of course, this advice needs to be tempered with your knowledge of what's customary in your industry. We talk about this in more detail in "Prospects Will Judge a Book By Its Cover" on page 73. Don't get too far outside what is customary, whether

> *"There is only one way under high heaven to get anybody to do anything ... and that is by making the other person want to do it."*
> —Dale Carnegie

Most Effective Prospecting Strategies

- Small forums/roundtables
- Speaking
- Being published
- Association activities
- Networking/referrals
- E-mail newsletters
- Paid seminars

Least effective prospecting strategies:

- Publicity (general)
- Direct mail
- Advertising
- Sponsoring events
- Brochures
- Unsolicited DVDs
- Cold calling

Source: Henry DeVries, founder of New Client Marketing Institute and author of Seducing the Client

it's too casual or too formal. That will create an uneasy feeling on the part of your prospect.

The whole issue of appearance is not as easy as it used to be because the rules of acceptable business dress have changed dramatically over the last few decades. Generation X and Y workers tend to be more casual than their older counterparts. Also, there are often regional influences on business dress that should be considered and respected. If you are an older person calling on younger prospects or vice versa, get advice from people who are in the demographic you need to relate to. This is an area where intuition plays a key role. If you're unsure, a conservative approach is usually best.

· *Work longer, smarter, and harder than your competitors.* Your prospects and customers will be able to see the results of your efforts.

Prospecting

Prospecting is the collection of proactive steps you take to identify and isolate qualified potential customers so you can either get in front of them or get them in front of you. There are two methods of prospecting: Pull, which attracts prospects to you through methods such as proper positioning, networking, or gaining industry-specific celebrity status; and push, which involves proactively contacting prospects one at a time on an individual basis through methods such as cold calling, phone solicitation, e-mail, letters, notes and so on.

Push methods are more time-consuming and often not as productive as the pull methods. It's more difficult to build trust and rapport with push methods, especially cold calling and phone solicitations, because you don't know what the prospect's needs are and many prospects will view you as an interruption. Pull methods of prospecting are generally more fruitful and profitable because they give you an opportunity to build value before you ever speak with a prospect. With pull methods, the fact that a prospect has initiated the contact gives you an advantage from the very beginning. In fact, studies show that 80 percent of sales in today's market take place when the buyer finds the seller, rather than the seller finding the buyer. This is largely due to the internet and the fact that it's so easy for customers to do their product and source research before they speak to a salesperson.

The major downside to pull prospecting is that you'll get a certain amount of price shoppers—the people who are focused exclusively on getting the lowest price. Your goal is to identify these prospects and don't waste too much time on them. Remember the

What Your Car Says About You

Your vehicle is as important to your appearance as your clothes. You may think it doesn't matter because you meet with your customers in their offices, but you never know when they are going to see your car—even if it's just through the window of their office. And though it's not common, customers have been known to walk outside with a salesperson after a meeting.

A dirty, messy car is going to reflect poorly on you. Keep it clean, running well, and remove all trash and clutter from the interior daily. Beyond the general maintenance, your vehicle should be appropriate to your market. Salespeople who call on a diverse clientele may want to have more than one vehicle. For example, we know salespeople who drive pickup trucks when they are calling on customers at heavy industrial or construction sites but drive mid-level sedans when calling on the corporate office. It's a good idea to pass on the luxury car when you're working because that could send the message to your prospects that you're charging too much.

five qualifying characteristics we discussed in Strategy Four: You are looking for prospects who have an awareness that they have a need and a reasonably clear understanding of what that need is, the authority to buy and ability to pay, a sense of urgency, a receptiveness to developing trust and rapport, and a willingness to listen. A price shopper may have the first two characteristics but not the other three. Ask questions that will allow you to qualify prospects early. Generally speaking, prospects that come to you through a pull method will be more willing to answer your questions than those you contact through a push method.

> *"You do not have to be superhuman to do what you believe in."*
> —Debbi Fields

Your own individual prospecting will usually be closely tied to your company's overall marketing efforts. It's important that you stay on top of the company's marketing strategies so you aren't surprised by anything that the company does in the way of advertising, promotion, public relations or other marketing. Also, periodically check your company's website so that you know what your customers and prospects see when they visit it.

Pre-Call Planning

Every sales call should be planned. That's every call, not just some or even most. And when you plan, overlook nothing. Assume nothing.

There is absolutely no room for shortcuts when it comes to pre-call planning. Salespeople who practice thorough pre-call planning are successful and rank in the top performers even when their presentation skills and sales talent is average. The number-one fear salespeople have is not missing the sale; it's being embarrassed in front of a customer. It's being asked a question they can't answer. It's being put on the spot where they look unprepared or foolish.

Professional salespeople will make sure that doesn't happen. They do everything in their power to prepare as well as they can.

Ask any salesperson about memorable moments in their career, and they'll usually think—if not talk—about the times when they were surprised, embarrassed, or in some way unprepared for something that occurred on a sales call. For high achievers, these moments are rare because they learn from their mistakes.

Another benefit of pre-call planning is that well-prepared salespeople are also more confident. The old tongue-twister "prior proper planning prevents poor performance" is true in just about any circumstance but especially so in sales. Certainly thorough product knowledge is critical—a salesperson should never get in front of a customer without it. But equally important is knowing the prospect, which is why you should find out as much as you can about the prospect *before* the call. Places to look for this information include:

- *Internet.* We've already discussed the internet as a rich resource, but it's worth repeating. Review your prospect's website carefully. Most websites have an "about us" page that gives an overview of the company. Many also have information on the company's history, founders, current management team, and goals for the future. If the site has a press room, be sure to read the posted press releases to see what kind of information the company is dispensing to the public. Once you've looked at the prospect's site, search for mentions of that company on various other sites using one or more of the major search engines.

- *Company annual reports.* The annual reports of public companies are public information. You can usually get a copy from the company by clicking on the "investor relations" link on its website. Most companies have this document available in a downloadable pdf format; if not, you can request that they send you a copy. Another option to get annual reports is www.annualreports.com, which is a free online directory of annual reports. You can also visit the U.S. Securities and Exchange Commission website at sec.gov for annual reports and other filings by public companies.

· *Trade journals, magazines, or newspapers with articles about your prospect.* A significant percentage of these articles should be available online and will be found during your internet research. Some publications require a subscription for you to access their materials; you'll have to make the decision about whether or not to make that investment based on the industry and what other information you are able to locate.

· *People your prospects sell to or buy from.* You can learn a lot from a prospect's customers and suppliers. At least some of these people are likely to be involved in industry associations, and you can meet them through networking. Some companies will list their customers on their websites as part of their credibility efforts; check to see if you recognize any of their customers and possibly know any of them.

· *People who have any sort of interaction with your prospect.* This varies tremendously by industry, of course, and may require some out-of-the-box thinking to come up with resources. You may have a friend, neighbor, someone you play sports with, go to church or volunteer with who has information you can use.

· *People who work at the prospect's place of business.* Think beyond the person who is the actual decision-maker when it comes to purchasing your product or service to anyone who might work there and be able to give you some insight. This person might also develop into an internal advocate for you.

· *The prospect's current and former customers.* Customers can be a tremendous resource because they can tell you what the company does right—and wrong. Those details may help you develop a picture of the company's needs and how they

relate to what you have to offer. It's possible that some of your existing customers are also customers of your prospect; if so, they'll likely be glad to help you in your research.

· *Prospect's internal newsletters or public documents.* Employee newsletters can tell you a lot about a company's operations and plans, although they may not be readily available to those outside the company. Be creative as you think about what other public documents you can use. Again, this will

Three Essential Steps Before Every Appointment

Make every sales call as fruitful as possible by taking these steps before each call:

1. *Confirm the appointment.* Call the day before to be sure there have been no schedule changes and the prospect is still expecting you. If you're seeing a customer you know well, you may do your confirmation by e-mail, but it's generally better to do this by phone so you can get a commitment.

2. *Mentally prepare yourself.* Engage in some positive self-talk and see yourself in the best possible way. Performance is a self-fulfilling prophecy. If you see yourself making a mistake, you probably will. Instead, visualize yourself performing at your absolute best and achieving the results you desire.

3. *Physically prepare yourself.* Make sure you are well-rested, relaxed, and content. Don't allow yourself to be tense, upset, agitated, or frustrated. Preparation helps eliminate tension and anxiety and will enhance your overall sense of well-being.

vary by industry. For example, if you sell food-service equipment, you may want to look at a restaurant's latest health or fire inspection report. If the prospect is a relatively new company, take a look at the articles of incorporation it filed with the state.

> *"Nobody's a natural. You work hard to get good and then work hard to get better."*
> —Paul Coffey

- *Prospect's technical manual or warranty documents.* Often these items can be found online and reveal information about how a company operates and issues it must deal with.
- *Prospect's marketing and promotional materials.* Always look at the prospect's marketing materials. Most will likely be on the company's website, but you also want to check out print and broadcast advertisements and any other materials you can find. This will give you an idea of how the company is positioned—or wants to be positioned—in the marketplace.

Know Who You Are Calling On

In addition to researching the company, find out as much as you can about the individual you will be calling on. Is this person an actual decision-maker or a decision-influencer? Does he or she have the authority to make the purchase or will someone else need to be consulted? Who else will have to be involved in the process? Just because the person is not the actual decision-maker does not necessarily mean you don't want to call on him. The company may have a system in place that requires you to follow a particular sequence of contacts in the sales process. Take care that you do not offend any of the decision-influencers on your way to the decision-maker.

> *"You have to perform at a consistently higher level than others. That's the mark of a true professional."*
> —Joe Paterno

You also want to know who you are competing against. This information may be available from some of the resources you'll use in researching the company. Your preparation should also include trying to determine what your prospect is going to want to know before making a decision. What is your prospect looking for in terms of outcomes or solutions? What problem can you help your prospect solve?

Plan Before Every Call

Is it possible to find out all of the information you need before your very first sales call on a company? Perhaps, but not likely. That's why pre-call planning before *every* call is absolutely essential. Don't plan before the first call and just wing the subsequent ones. You may adjust your pre-call planning strategy based on how well you've gotten to know the prospect and what you need to accomplish on a specific call, but you can never ignore this critical step of the sales process.

Respect the Gatekeepers

A gatekeeper is anyone you must go through to get to the decision-maker. Gatekeepers are typically receptionists, secretaries, and assistants, but they could also be a first-line manager or other decision-influencer. Many salespeople tend to view gatekeepers either as unimportant or as another obstacle to overcome on the way to the sale—or, if the gatekeeper is really strong, as an insurmountable barrier. We recommend you make the gatekeeper your ally.

Here's a story that illustrates the benefit of that: Several years ago, a chemical salesperson wanted to find out more about a new prospect, a manufacturing facility in a small South Carolina town. He was in the area so he decided to stop in and ask the receptionist about setting an appointment with the decision-maker. We want to stress that he wasn't cold calling with the goal of making a sales call, he was cold calling as a prospecting tool. He didn't want to see the decision-maker that day, he wanted to meet the gatekeeper and find out some information about how the company's purchasing process operated. It turned out that the receptionist, a crusty old lady, was definitely the gatekeeper for the decision-maker, and she took her job very seriously. When the salesperson presented his card and told her why he was there, she said, "No one gets to see him except through me, and I don't believe you should see him." Then she tore his card in half and dropped it in the trashcan.

He was shocked, but he kept his wits enough to politely thank her, and he left. A lot of other salespeople would have simply given up or perhaps tried to circumvent the gatekeeper. Not this one. He drove to the next town, found a florist, and sent her a bouquet of flowers. On the note, he wrote: "Thank you for being a consummate professional. I can tell that you are very loyal and dedicated."

After the flowers were delivered, she called him. She said: "I've got two things to say to you. First, I had to dig through the trash to find your business card that I tore up to get your phone number. Second, I received your flowers, and I know exactly what you are trying to do. And it worked."

She may have been rude, but she wasn't stupid—she knew that the line about being a consummate professional was patronizing, but she appreciated the fact that he respected her position and didn't try to go around her nor did he try to do battle with her. She later told him that no one had ever done anything like that before. And yes, she did set up a meeting for him with the plant manager and that company became an excellent account for the salesperson.

Not all gatekeepers will be so blatant in their blocking techniques. But it's important to understand that the gatekeeper's job is to protect their boss's time. Certainly some gatekeepers might

overstep their limits of authority, but most of them are doing what they are told to do, which is screening the people who want to see their bosses. If you take the time to befriend them, show them that you have something of benefit, and gain their support, they will not only allow you access to the decision-maker, they will do it in a way that gives you an advantage over your competition.

Now that we've told you how one salesperson successfully dealt with a blocking gatekeeper, we'll tell you about one who will likely never get to the prospect he'd like to reach.

When I (JK Harris) was working on my first book, *Flashpoint: Seven Core Strategies for Rapid-Fire Business Growth*, I created the Flashpoints brand and Flashpoints Consulting, LLC. I retained Jacquelyn Lynn to, among other things, manage the brand, produce the Flashpoints newsletter, and choose suppliers for whatever we need. I trust her judgment and gave her complete autonomy.

She received an e-mail from a casual acquaintance who has a company whose services include publishing books for authors who choose not to go with traditional publishers. The e-mail requested an introduction to me. Jacquelyn has introduced me to a number of people with whom I have developed productive relationships, so she doesn't automatically block everyone, but she is selective. She knows that I'm very busy, and she is careful not to waste my time. So she looked at this young man's website to verify the services he was offering, determined that Flashpoints didn't need any of them, and sent him a very professional e-mail reply. In it, she explained her position with the company, told him that we have a long-term contract with Entrepreneur Press to publish and distribute the books in the Flashpoints series and that we had no need for any of the other services he offered, but if that should change in the future, we would certainly keep him in mind. So he sent an e-mail directed to me through our website—a friendly, chatty, "let's get together and have coffee sometime" message.

His first mistake was that in both his initial e-mail and his subsequent one, he didn't clearly state even one benefit he could offer to me or Flashpoints. His second mistake was that he didn't bother to acknowledge her e-mail; he should have at least thanked her for taking the time to write back, but he didn't. His third mistake was that after she wrote to him, he tried to go around her and get to me by sending an e-mail through the general mailbox on the Flashpoints website (theflashpoints.com). E-mail to that address goes to her, but apparently he didn't realize that. I appreciate persistence and creativity; I'm not impressed by unprofessionalism and discourtesy or people who want to waste my time. My gatekeepers—as are the gatekeepers of every decision-maker you'll ever call on—are in place for a reason. When you show a lack of respect to a gatekeeper, you are showing a lack of respect for the decision-maker.

Leverage Your Time and Resources

In financial terms, leverage is defined as the use of a small initial investment to gain a very high return in relation to that investment, to control a much larger investment, or to reduce your liability for any loss. In general terms, leverage is the power or ability to act or influence people, events, and decisions.

There are only four ways to leverage your time and resources. One is to invest them, in which case you'll get something back. The second is to spend them, and you may or may not get something back. The third is to waste them, which means you don't expect a return. And the fourth is to abuse them, which is to intentionally waste your time and resources.

Savvy salespeople know that the way to leverage their time and resources for maximum results is to invest them. Time and energy invested, for example, in pre-call planning and prospect research will produce results. Time and energy spent on cold calling may or may not pay off. Time and energy wasted with minimally qualified prospects is likely to provide minimal, if any, return—and it's an abuse of your time and energy to intentionally waste it with an unqualified prospect.

Time is your most valuable asset. Once it's gone, it's gone— you can never get it back. Leverage every minute of your time for maximum results.

KEY LESSONS

* Positioning is how you and your organization are seen in the marketplace. Branding is the emotional side of how you, your company and products are perceived in the market.

* Common positioning mistakes include: relying too much on cold calling; being too pushy; appearing desperate; presenting yourself as the stereotypical, fast-talking salesperson; immediately dropping your price; and being a product-pusher.

* Close to 90 percent of today's buyers have already researched what they want on the internet, and they often know more about it than the salespeople calling on them. Don't expect to be perceived as an authority unless you truly are.

* Top professionals position themselves as industry experts by researching and joining the organizations their customers belong to; reading the same journals, trade publications, and other materials their customers read; regularly searching the internet for industry information and trends; gathering as much information as possible about the competition; asking other salespeople for insight on industry trends, common customer concerns, and other ideas; dressing one notch above the prospect or customers; and working longer, smarter, and harder than their competitors.

* Spend your time carefully planning your activities and quali-

fying prospects. Don't waste time trying to sell to unqualified prospects.

* The four key people you need to identify at any prospect are the internal advocate, the check writer, the decision-maker, and the user.

* Your direct value statement is a 30-second speech that tells people what you do in a way that will make them ask for more information.

* Always remember what's going through your prospect's mind at your first meeting—it's likely he's wondering who you are, who you represent, and what's in it for him if he agrees to see you.

* Prospecting is what you do to identify and isolate potential customers. The two methods of prospecting are pull, which attracts prospects to you, and push, which means you contact the prospects. Push methods are more time-consuming than and often not as productive as pull methods. Studies show that 80 percent of sales in today's market take place when the buyer finds the seller (pull) rather than the seller finding the buyer (push).

* Your vehicle is as important to your image as your clothes. Keep your car well-maintained, free of clutter, and clean inside and out.

* Plan thoroughly before every sales call. The number-one fear of salespeople is being embarrassed in front of a customer; pre-call planning can prevent that from happening.

* Find out as much as you can about a prospect before the call. Places to look for information include the internet; company annual reports; trade journals, magazines, or newspapers; peo-

ple your prospects sell to or buy from; people who have any sort of interaction with your prospect; people who work at the prospect's place of business; the prospect's current and former customers; the prospect's internal newsletters and public documents; the prospect's technical manual or warranty documents; the prospect's marketing and promotional materials.

✳ The three essential steps you should take before every appointment are confirm the appointment, mentally prepare yourself, and physically prepare yourself.

✳ Treat gatekeepers with courtesy and respect.

Get in Sync with Your Prospect

The second step of the IMPACT sales system is *meet*. The purpose of this step is to build trust and rapport, gain a better understanding of your prospect, develop a dialogue with the prospect, and set the sales process in motion. During this step, you should be able to measure your prospect's willingness to engage with you and begin the sales process.

The purpose of the meet step is *not* to sell yourself. It is not to talk about your product. It is not to dominate the conversation, interrupt the prospects, or even to get them to like you. It is to set the stage so the prospects feel comfortable and are willing to share their situation in such a way that you can gain an understanding of whether or not you can be a solution for what their particular issue may be.

> *"When dealing with people, remember you are not dealing with creatures of logic, but creatures of emotion."*
>
> —Dale Carnegie

You only have a matter of seconds—in fact, studies show you have from 19 to 34 seconds—to establish your credibility and convince a prospect that time spent with you will be valuable. In these seconds, you must answer the questions that are going through your prospect's mind, whether he's thinking them consciously or unconsciously. Those questions are: Who are you? Why are you here? What do you want? What's in it for me? And that last one is critical.

The Value of Trust

Developing trust is critical. Without trust, you can only sell price, and that never works long-term. With trust, you can sell value.

When prospects don't trust you, they're not going to allow you to continue the sales process. They'll stop you at the beginning, perhaps by throwing out a price objection or some other objection that will cause you to stumble. It's their way of letting you know that they're feeling uncomfortable with you. Without trust, every price is too high—yet without trust, the only sales strategy you have is price. But price is not an effective way to sell. When you have trust, you have the opportunity to build value around the price or build value for the price you charge.

If you have adequately conducted pre-call planning activities and you understand who you are going to see, you have a strong knowledge of the industry and the prospect, you know what issues you may be able to help with, and you have scheduled an appointment, your trust factor will be higher from the moment you first meet the prospect. It will be easier for you to find out what you need to know to continue the sales process.

It's important to understand that there is a significant difference between building trust and being liked. Certainly it's important to be liked. If you're not liked, you can't get in the door. But though liking may get you in the door, it won't keep you there. To get fully in the room, not just through the door, you need to build trust. It's not enough that people like you—people can like you and still not trust you.

> *"It's critically important for salespeople to be able to think on their feet, especially in the heat of the battle when prospects are likely to say unexpected things."*
>
> —Richard D. Dickerson

The Source of Buyers' Mistrust

Everyone has a story to tell about being misled, coerced, or manipulated by a salesperson. It's no wonder that prospects are often initially suspicious and wary of salespeople. Building trust takes time, effort, and the creation of consistent experiences. It helps to understand the feelings and perceptions that are well-entrenched in most prospects. They are:

1. *Fear of making a buying mistake.* Buyers are often afraid they'll pay too much or too little, buy out of fear instead of genuine need, or not get what they truly need or want.

2. *Fear of looking stupid.* Those fears include succumbing to pressure, being "suckered," falling for a "pitch," buying to get rid of a pushy salesperson, and purchasing only because the prospect "liked" the salesperson.

3. *Fear of being criticized or ridiculed.* We don't want friends and associates to make fun of us for a buying decision.

Recognize the source of your prospects' mistrust and focus on overcoming those feelings by building trust and value.

It's not necessarily that they *dis*trust you, it's that they don't know you well enough to trust you. But if you're going to achieve a successful sales result, you want your prospects to believe that you, your organization, and your products are credible and will deliver on every promise or commitment. That's trust.

What's more, trust is a two-way street. Your prospects want to be trusted as well. Give them a chance to open up to you so that the trust can be mutual.

Remember that worrying about being liked is self-focused—it means you're worrying more about yourself than you are about your prospects and customers. Trust and rapport demonstrate a sincere commitment to your customers.

What Are Your Intentions?

One of the first things you should do in this step is to state your intentions. Tell the prospect what you want to accomplish. For example, you might say, "Hello, I'm George White from Super Manufacturing. As you know, the purpose of our appointment today is to get to know you better, to talk about Super Manufacturing's offerings, and to discuss anything you might like to discuss with me. If at any point in time you feel like we are not achieving that, please let me know." Then be quiet. Wait for a response. Most of the time, the response will be an agreement statement, such as "Fine," or "That's good." By doing this, you've set the tone for a professional meeting and let the prospect know that you respect his time and he is in charge.

A lot of salespeople have trouble at this point because they walk in and don't know what to say—and that makes it difficult for them to get on the right track with the entire meeting. It's a major hurdle. Starting with small talk is one of the worst ways to begin, unless you know the customer and know for certain that he likes small talk. Most buyers—whether they are at the C-level, mid-level purchasing agents, or individual consumers—want you to get to the point and not waste their time. At the same time, they are offended when a salesperson immediately begins talking about the product's features and benefits without first identifying the needs and wants.

Some sales training programs recommend starting with an icebreaker by looking around a prospect's office and commenting on something you see. That would be appropriate *after* you have established trust and rapport, not before or even as a way to establish trust. Think about it: Are you comfortable when someone you've just met in a business situation starts making personal comments? Yes, people put pictures, mementos, and other items around their offices because they represent things that are of interest to them, but that doesn't necessarily mean they want to talk about them with a salesperson they aren't sure they trust yet. Save the personal chitchat for later meetings.

Remember, there is a natural distrust of salespeople that you must overcome if you are going to take your meeting to a successful conclusion. Our research has clearly shown that the least offensive way to open a sales call is with a statement of intention that tells the prospect why you are there, that you want an open dialogue, and that you don't want to be presumptuous about anything. Note that we say "least offensive" and not "best." There are no openings that prospects view as great or even good. Most prospects are prepared to be offended to some degree by salespeople because it's something that has happened so often they've come to expect it. But they are least offended by a salesperson who introduces himself and clearly and succinctly states the purpose of the meeting at the outset.

This portion of your sales call should not take more than 30 seconds. If it does, you will lose the prospect and position yourself as a stereotypical peddler. You don't have to use the exact words in our example, but we know from research and experience that it's the best model. Adjust it to fit your situation—for example, you may have learned something when you were setting up the appointment that may be appropriate to mention. The key is to keep your statement customer-focused, encourage dialogue, and make sure the prospect knows he is going to be heard.

By making a statement of intention, you are beginning to establish trust. You are beginning to penetrate the invisible barrier that's always there for every buyer and seller in the early stages. You want to get rid of that barrier, and in order to do that, you have to build as much trust as possible. Remember, people want to buy, they don't want to be sold. You have to build a relationship in which your prospects do not feel like you're just there to sell them something.

Skip the Data Dump

Salespeople should be excited about their products. If they're not, they need to find something else to sell. But don't get so excited about what you have to offer that you walk into a sales call and start unloading with features, benefits, and jazzy presentations without first getting in sync with your prospect. Do you buy from people who unload on you with no apparent concern for what you want and need? We don't—and we don't know anybody who does. Yet we still see it going on in sales calls all the time. Don't do it.

The Key to a Great First Impression

We don't have to tell you about the importance of making a good first impression, but when it comes to first impressions, be aware that how you look is more important than what you say. Research indicates that nonverbal cues carry up to four times more weight than what is actually spoken. Your words (your statement of intention) will let your prospect know about your future actions, but your nonverbal cues will offer insight into who you are as a person.

Prospects will notice your facial expression; your ability to maintain eye contact; how you stand, sit, and walk; the tone of your voice; and, of course, the way you are dressed. First impressions are usually formed in less than 30 seconds—and the ones formed from nonverbal cues are extremely accurate.

When you like someone initially, you will look for additional reasons to like them more as you go along. Your prospects do the same thing. But if that first impression is negative, people will generally focus on more things that will make them dislike the other person. It can take up to six months to overcome a bad first impression—can you afford to work six months just to recover from a bad beginning?

Before you meet every prospect, first find a mirror and check your appearance—because your prospect will do exactly that. If the prospect's office is in a building with a restroom in a public area, take advantage of it. If not, say something like this to the receptionist: "I have an appointment with Mr. Smith, but before you announce me, may I please use your restroom?"

When you meet the prospect, offer a genuine smile that sends a message that you are friendly and not a threat. Make your handshake firm, not a bone-crusher or a dead-fish type of shake. Speak clearly. Look your prospect in the eye—that's one eye, preferably the right one. If you allow your eyes to shift back and forth between your prospect's right and left eye, you will look "shifty-eyed" and untrustworthy. If you are invited to sit down, do so—but sit up straight and lean forward to show enthusiasm and interest in the other person. These first few seconds are the most important part of a sales call; be sure to treat them that way.

Be Ready for Anything

One of the exciting things about sales as a profession is that it's always interesting. Anything can—and often will—happen on a sales call. That's why you have to be able to think on your feet and not be thrown when something unexpected happens.

In most cases, the unexpected will be in the form of something the prospect says. A salesperson for a motor freight company tells the story of meeting a prospect for the first time. She had spoken with him briefly on the phone to set the appointment, and that conversation had been strictly business. When she arrived at his office and was announced by the receptionist, he came out to the reception area to greet her. As he approached, he loudly asked, "Are you carrying a gun?" She was surprised but quickly responded with, "No, should I be?" He laughed and said, "I thought all of you trucking company reps were highway robbers, and I just wondered if you were armed or not."

It was a tasteless and not particularly funny joke that demeaned the sales profession. But just because a customer says something offensive doesn't mean you should respond in kind. In this case, the salesperson simply smiled, held up her hands and said, "No weapons. But maybe I should give that approach a try." Then she segued into her statement of intention, and the call proceeded in a professional manner.

A salesperson for a bedding company tells the story of a couple who came into his store to shop for a new bed. To help someone choose the right bed, the salesperson needs to know a few things about their sleeping habits. This salesperson typically asked prospects if they had children who sometimes slept with them or might get in bed with them in the morning, or if they allowed their pets to sleep with them because these issues would influence the size and type of bed he would recommend. So it was a routine question when he asked the couple, "Does anyone ever get in the bed with you?" Expecting a response relating to either kids or dogs, he was shocked when the husband answered, "I've been trying to get her to do that for years, but she just won't." On another occasion, this same salesperson had his sense of tact tested when a very overweight customer sat down on the edge of a bed in the showroom and the bed collapsed.

Customers can—and do—say just about anything, so be prepared. Some will deliberately try to shock you because they want to throw you off your game. Don't let them. Others aren't trying to distract you, but they'll still do things that have that potential effect. And there will always be things beyond the control of both you and your prospects. Expect that, and keep your wits about you.

Should You Learn a Script?

At The Brooks Group, we often joke that we don't teach scripts because the customers don't remember their lines. Seriously, we know that people typically don't buy from a salesperson who sounds scripted. They want to have a conversation, not sit through a performance. Of course, even though we don't suggest memorizing scripts, we also believe there is no such thing as being over-prepared, and your preparation includes thinking about and practicing what you're going to say.

Consider actors in a live theater performance. You know they are saying lines they've memorized, the same lines that they say night after night after night, but if they are good actors, it always sounds fresh and natural. What's more, if something happens that's not in the script—a prop breaks, another character flubs his lines, there is unexpected noise from the audience—good actors are able to ad lib their way back to the script without breaking character and usually without anyone realizing that something went wrong. That's the approach you need to take when you're selling: Know your material so well that it's intuitive and second nature.

I (Richard Dickerson) occasionally travel with the salespeople we train, and I work with them one-on-one in the field as they learn the IMPACT system. I was once in Pennsylvania with a salesperson and we were calling on the CEO of a large paper company. We agreed in advance that she was going to introduce me as a consultant who was riding with her without mentioning that I was a sales trainer.

We got into the CEO's office, and she began her statement of intention. As we explained earlier, the statement of intention simply explains why you are there and begins the trust building process. You may also choose to follow your statement of intention with a bonding statement, which we'll explain in Strategy Seven. We recommend a general format for these statements, but they shouldn't be memorized. And what happened on that call with the CEO of the paper company is a perfect example of why.

This salesperson began her statement of intention by saying: "You know, the purpose of our meeting today is to talk to you because I understand what kind of work you do." And then she stopped, looked at me, and said, "Wait a minute, that's not right, is it?"

She had tried to memorize her statement of intention but forgot her lines. I told her to keep going, but she was so flustered that she started crying. The CEO was very understanding and suggested that she just start over. She tried, but she was so upset she just couldn't get it right. Finally the CEO said, "I'll tell you what: Just tell me how you think you can help me." We ended up being there for about an hour and a half; he agreed to buy some things from her and asked her to come back when she was calmer.

> *"My father said: 'You must never try to make all the money that's in a deal. Let the other fellow make some money too, because if you have a reputation for always making all the money, you won't have many deals.'"*
>
> —J. Paul Getty

When she and I got out to the car, she said, "I can't believe I did that" and started to fall apart again. I told her that she just needed to relax. She had

Don't Waste Time with Small Talk

Top salespeople talk about things that are important and relevant to their prospects. If the prospects want to engage in small talk, that's fine. But if they don't, sharp salespeople get straight to the point and tell prospects what they'd like to accomplish and why.

In a study conducted by The Brooks Group, 95 percent of CEOs found unsolicited small talk that was initiated by the salesperson to be negative or, at best, neutral. The point here is that when the salesperson initiates the small talk, it's not well-received. If the prospect initiates the small talk, go along with it. Just remember that it's very difficult to move from social chat to a sales discussion; it's much easier to go the other way. So reserve your social chitchat for a more appropriate time because you are there to talk about providing the solution your prospect wants.

been so focused on getting the script correct that she got herself in trouble because she wasn't paying attention to the customer. She was more concerned about showing me that she had learned the system and was using all the elements than she was on making a sale. She was fortunate that the CEO was a very kind, compassionate man.

So should you learn a script? No—but you should know your material so well that you automatically and intuitively say the right thing at the right time. That's thinking on your feet.

Your Behavior Style

An issue strongly related to the process of building trust and rapport is understanding your own behavior style and how it interacts with others. What is your dominant behavior style? Do you tend to be extroverted or introverted? Now, what about your prospects or customers? What have you noticed about their behavior style?

The most successful salespeople have learned to mirror the style of their customers because the simple truth is that people like to buy from those who are most like themselves. It enhances the trust, and they feel better about the process.

However—and this is critical—you need to be careful to mirror, not mimic. There is a big difference. People will notice if you mimic, and they'll be offended.

Interact with people in the way their style indicates they will be most receptive to you. The old saying that you should treat people like you want to be treated is not true. You should treat people like *they* want to be treated. Change the Golden Rule of "Do unto others as you would have them do unto you," to "Do unto others as *they* would have you do unto them." See the difference? And to do that, you have to pay attention to their styles.

If your buyer or prospect is very extroverted and you tend to be more introverted, you need to boost your energy level and be more outgoing. If you don't, you'll hinder your communication with that person, and that will diminish your trust factor. On the other hand, if you are high-energy and strongly extroverted but your prospect is more low-keyed and introverted, you need to tone it down. You want to respond to your prospects in a way that is most appropriate for them.

This is crucial to building trust and rapport. That's why you need to mirror, not mimic. And it's entirely possible your prospect will recognize what you're trying to do, and if so, that's fine. The key is that you do not appear to be extreme, fake, or contrived because that destroys trust. This is not in any

> *"Don't rush to the close. If you get to the close without first having established trust, you either won't make the sale, or you will make the sale but the buyer will cancel."*
>
> —JK Harris

way deceitful or manipulative; it is simply you presenting yourself so that your prospect is most likely to communicate openly with you.

———— KEY LESSONS ————

* When you meet a prospect, your goal is to build trust and rapport, gain a better understanding of your prospect, develop a dialogue, and set the sales process in motion.

* Developing trust with a prospect is critical. Without trust, you can only sell price. With trust, you can sell value.

* If you're going to achieve a successful sales result, your prospects must believe that you, your organization, and your products are credible and will deliver on every promise or commitment.

* Buyers are afraid of making a buying mistake, looking stupid, and being criticized or ridiculed. Focus on overcoming these feelings by building trust and value.

* The first thing you should do when you meet a prospect is to make a statement of intention so the prospect knows why you are there and what you want to accomplish, yet still feels in control of the meeting.

* Don't waste time talking about things the prospect has not expressed an interest in.

* Remember that first impressions are formed within the first 30 seconds. Check your appearance and mannerisms to be sure your first impression will be positive.

* Learn how to think on your feet so you are not rattled when the unexpected happens.

✳ Don't memorize a script—just know your material so well that you automatically and intuitively say the right thing at the right time.

✳ People like to buy from people who are like themselves, so mirror the style of your prospects.

✳ Change the Golden Rule of "Do unto others as you would have them do unto you," to "Do unto others as *they* would have you do unto them."

Identify a Prospect's True Needs

The third step of the IMPACT system is *probing,* which is really the sales interview. It's the time where you identify the prospect's reason for buying, as well as how, what, when, and under what conditions he'll buy. To do this successfully, you must provide value to your prospect. And to deliver value, you must see yourself primarily as a value resource. You accomplish that by first discovering what the prospect perceives as value. You must probe to uncover the prospect's true needs and wants, and determine the issues that will affect a buying decision. The best way to serve your own interests is to put the needs, problems, and issues of your customers first.

We use the term *probe* to fit with the IMPACT acronym, but this doesn't mean you're poking at your prospect with a sharp stick—either literally or figuratively. This is an interview, not an inquisition. It's a conversation. You want to ask questions so you can gather the information you need, and you want to do it in a way that will make the prospect comfortable and willing to answer you. Remember, you must sustain the trust you established in the *meet* step.

Tips for Success in the Probe Step

The first step is to ask permission to ask questions and also to make notes of the prospect's answers. This is one of the most powerful sales success tips we can offer. It's so simple and basic, yet so many salespeople don't bother to do it—they just jump in asking questions, and suddenly it's not a conversation, it's an interrogation. No wonder prospects get their guard up and are reluctant to give honest, complete answers! A simple permission request tells prospects that you respect them and that you're not going to do anything without them knowing about it and approving it. It will help you maintain and expand on the trust you have begun building.

The permission step can be combined with the intention statement we discussed in Strategy Six, and it's very simple and straightforward. You might say, "Before I tell you about Super Manufacturing, I'd like to ask you a few questions so I understand exactly what your needs are and can recommend some possible solutions. I'd like to make a few notes so I don't miss anything that's important to you, or misunderstand anything. Is that okay?" You've just set the stage to let the prospect do most of the talking and avoid unsolicited small talk.

On the surface, this sounds like one of those no-brainers that's almost a waste of time. No one who has agreed to see you is going to say no to this request. Even so, you still need to do it. As we've said, simply plunging into your questions is likely to be off-putting at the minimum and will likely raise the barrier that naturally exists between salespeople and prospects. Asking permission prepares the prospect for your questions, obtains his consent to ask, increases trust, and chips away at that barrier. It also gives the prospect a chance to set some ground rules, perhaps establishing some confidentiality parameters or time constraints.

It's not enough to get permission to ask questions—you also want to get permission to make notes. Think about how you would feel if you were talking to a salesperson who suddenly starting writing things down. You would probably wonder what was being written down and why. It would likely distract you and make you feel uncomfortable. But if the salesperson essentially says, "I want to write down the things you say because they're important, I want to be sure to understand them, and I want to remember them," before starting to take notes, you're not surprised, and you won't be put off when the note-taking starts.

Here's an essential point: When you ask for permission to take notes, be sure you take them! It is easy to forget, to get so wrapped up in what the prospect is saying that you forget to write things down. And if they are speaking rapidly or giving you a lot of statistical data, you may need to ask them to pause for a moment so you can get it all. All you have to do is say something like, "Can you give me a second? I need to write this down." Most people will not mind pausing. And if you're not sure you got everything accurately, ask for clarification and confirmation. Say, "I want to be sure I understood you. You said [repeat what you have in your notes]. Is that accurate?"

You'll want to refer to your notes as you move through the sales interview and are ready to make a recommendation. Your notes will summarize what the prospect is trying to accomplish, and you won't have to rely exclusively on your memory.

Another benefit of the statement of intention coupled with the permission request is that it allows you to easily move the prospect through the steps of the sales process. It looks like the table on page 106.

Statement of Intention→	Meet Step→	Probe Step→	Apply Step
"The purpose of our appointment today is …"	"… to get to know you better …"	"… ask you a few questions …"	"… recommend some possible solutions …"

We cannot stress enough that you should not start asking questions until you have permission to do so. Opening questions, such as "What would you like to accomplish in your business?" or "What are the biggest problems you're facing in production?" are likely to be viewed as intrusive and presumptuous—unless you've told the prospect you want to ask questions, and he has agreed to allow you to do that. Also, your questions should be genuine efforts to identify the prospect's wants and needs, not manipulative efforts to get him to say yes. For example, if you ask questions such as "Are you looking for ways to save money?" or "Is increasing productivity important to you?," the prospect will likely say "yes" out loud but be thinking to himself that it's a stupid question—after all, who doesn't want to save money and increase productivity?—and you're just trying to manipulate him.

> *"If Columbus had turned back, no one would have blamed him. Of course, no one would have remembered him either."*
>
> —Unknown

Follow Intention with Bonding

With your statement of intention and permission request, incorporate a bonding statement that shows that you understand both your prospects and their businesses. If you were meeting with a CEO, you might say something like: "As we discussed on the

phone, the purpose of our appointment today is to get to know you better, to talk about Super Manufacturing's offerings, and to discuss anything you might like to discuss with me. I would really appreciate it if at any time I seem off course, please let me know. [Pause long enough for an acknowledgment, then move to the bonding statement.] I understand that, as a CEO, it's important that you call your own shots and be in charge of your day-to-day operations. Do you mind if I ask you some questions around those activities?"

Adjust your bonding statement to match the level of the prospect in the corporate hierarchy. If you're meeting with a manager, your bonding statement could sound like this: "I understand how important it is to be in charge and run your operation smoothly with no problems or issues. Do you mind if I ask you some questions?" Another alternative is this general version of a bonding statement: "I have learned over the years that when people get exactly what they're looking for in the way they want it, they are happiest and things work out best. Do you mind if I ask you some questions to see if we could do that?"

This is a non-threatening way to tell the prospect what you want to do, ask for his participation, and at the same time say, "I understand you and your business, and I respect how valuable your time is." People want to be understood, and they are more likely to trust someone who has taken the time and interest to understand them.

> *"The only way to know how customers see your business is to look at it through their eyes."*
> —Daniel R. Scroggin

We want to stress that the statement of intention that we discussed in Strategy Six and the bonding statement are two different things. They work hand-in-hand, but they are not the same. Though this entire process of stating your intentions, asking permission, and bonding may take less than a minute, it

When You're Not the Best Option

There are times when your best sales strategy is to walk away from a prospect. If during the probe step of the process you determine that your product or service isn't a true fit for the prospect's wants and needs, be honest and say so. If you happen to know of a better source, make a recommendation.

This is not the same thing as the manipulative closing technique known as the "take away" where you attempt to create desire for your product by making it unavailable, often with statements such as, "Only a small percentage of the people we talk with will qualify." This is what you should do when you realize that what you have to offer isn't the best option for your prospect. For example, at JK Harris & Company, we occasionally see prospective clients who owe relatively small amounts in back taxes. When what they owe is about the same or only slightly higher than what our fee to handle their case would be, we point that out upfront, suggest that they simply reach a payment arrangement with the IRS themselves, and provide them with the appropriate IRS contact information. Could we sell them on our services? Probably, but it wouldn't be the right thing to do.

When you are meeting with a prospect and it becomes apparent that your product isn't their best option, refer to your notes and summarize the situation. Say something like: "Based on what you've told me, you want these three things [and list them]. I wish I could provide that, but our product won't do what you want, and I don't want you to buy something from us that you won't be happy with. XYZ Company has a product that is more appropriate to your needs, so you might want to give them a call. I appreciate your time and if things change in the future, I hope you'll give me a chance to serve you then."

That "lost sale"—which isn't really a lost sale because it wasn't right in the first place—will come back to you many times over. Prospects will appreciate and remember that you acted with honesty and integrity.

has clearly separate elements that you need to understand for maximum effectiveness.

Pay Attention

Give prospects your undivided attention. That means focus on what they are saying, not on what you're going to ask next. Listen with your eyes, ears, heart, and soul. Never interrupt them but be interruptable—in other words, let them interrupt you if they choose. Ignore any external distractions. Try to control as many outside influences as possible. This should be fairly easy when the prospect is in your space but can be difficult when you're in the prospect's space. Even so, do the best you can. Specifically, turn your cell phone off—not just on vibrate but *completely off*, because it will distract you and the prospect may be able to hear the vibration and also be distracted. When you enter the prospect's office, offer to close the door. Don't just automatically do it; it's not your place to make that decision. But ask: "Would you like me to close the door?" That demonstrates respect for the prospect and your desire to focus on the subject of your meeting. Think about other things you can do that are appropriate to the physical situation in which you sell that can minimize or even remove external distractions and interruptions.

> "If there were no problems, most of us would be unemployed."
>
> —Zig Ziglar

Asking Questions

Once you've let prospects know that you need to ask questions to get the information you need to help them, you should be able to ask the right questions in the correct way. There are two types of questions: open-ended and closed-ended.

Open-ended questions require prospects to tell you how they feel, what they want, and what they think. These questions

typically begin with *how, what, who, when,* and *where.* Most of your questions, especially during the probe phase and even later when we move into Strategy Eight, which is the apply step, should be open-ended, reflective, and easy to answer. You want the prospect to do most of the talking.

Prepare your questions in advance. Write them down. When you receive permission to make notes of the prospect's answers, you have permission to break eye contact. That means you are able to look down at your prepared questions without any awkwardness so you can be sure you get all the information you need. It's as difficult to remember all the questions you need to ask as it is to remember all the answers.

Closed-ended questions require a simple "yes" or "no" response. Their purpose is to clearly define an option or interest, or to narrow a choice. Closed-ended questions typically begin with *do, is, are, would.* Use these questions sparingly because too many of them will discourage your prospect from talking and yield limited information. They can also set a negative tone.

Ask questions that are designed to get your prospects talking about their need for the benefits—not the features—of your product and to reveal their wants, which will often be different from their needs. Once the prospect answers you, follow up with more questions to get additional information.

Make your questions work together so your prospect feels like he is participating in a comfortable conversation rather than being the target of an inquisition.

Why Questions Are Important

Salespeople who don't know how to ask questions and listen will talk themselves out of more sales than they'll make. That's why it's important to hone your questioning skills. When you question correctly, you get beneath the surface to discover and reveal what's really going on in the prospect's mind and heart.

Here are ten reasons why the ability to ask good questions is so essential to a successful sales process:

1. Questions put the salesperson in control of the interaction, even though if the questions are properly asked the prospect will feel like he is in control.
2. Questions demonstrate that the salesperson is interested in learning more about the prospect and his business.
3. Questions allow salespeople to learn more.
4. Questions allow salespeople to engage the prospect and get him to do most of the talking.
5. Questions help salespeople find out when, how, what, and why a prospect will buy their product or service.
6. Questions prove the salesperson is more interested in learning about the prospect than in talking about his own concerns.
7. Questions give salespeople time to think.
8. Questions display professionalism and depth of interest.
9. Questions position salespeople as problem-solvers.
10. Questions prepare salespeople to present their product or service in the way the prospect wants to see it.

When you're the customer, don't you prefer it when the salesperson asks you questions to identify your true wants and needs before launching into a presentation—and then clearly keeps those wants and needs in mind as he talks about his product?

Consider this hypothetical situation: It's election season and you've gone to a meet-and-greet for local candidates. One candidate for city council offered a firm handshake, told you that he wanted to know what the voters were concerned about, and then asked you questions such as these: What do you like most about the community where you live? If you could change anything about that community, what would it be? What would you like to see your community do more of? Less of? What is the one thing that could make your community the best in the area?

Another candidate for the same office greets you and launches into what amounts to a speech, telling you about all the great things he's planning to do for your community if he's elected.

Which candidate are you likely to be more interested in learning more about and possibly voting for—the one who shows a genuine interest in your concerns or the one who already has all the answers? The problem with people who already have all the answers is that they may in fact have some great ideas, but without taking the time to find out what's on your mind, they could completely miss your biggest concerns. They're also not particularly interesting to have a conversation with because they're too busy talking to engage you in a meaningful exchange of ideas. And then there's the trust factor—who are you more likely to trust? Chances are, you'll put a lot more trust in the person with the questions.

Principles for Asking Good Questions

Good questions may sound spontaneous, but they're not. Here's how you can make your questions structured, well-delivered, well-timed, and correctly articulated:

- *Know exactly what you plan to ask before you ever get in front of a prospect.* Your questions should not sound canned or rehearsed, but you should know what they're going to be ahead of time.
- *Ask open-ended questions that give your prospects a chance to open up and offer information.*
- *Phrase your questions strategically so the prospect will share how he perceives his problems, needs, and expectations.*
- *Aim your questions at your prospect's dominant driver.* When you begin to notice a common thread in your prospect's answers, you are uncovering his dominant need, problem, or expectation. Aim your questions in that direction so you can deepen your understanding of how your product or

service can satisfy what the
prospect wants to accomplish.

> "The successful warrior is
> the average man, with
> laser-like focus."
>
> —Bruce Lee

- *Avoid offensive or insensitive questions.* This should go without saying, but it doesn't. Sometimes salespeople fail to consider what they're asking and how they're phrasing it. Think about how the question will be received before you ask.

- *Start broad and go narrow.* Broad questions tend to be less threatening, and they help you identify a direction for more focused questions.

- *Speak simply and avoid jargon.* Don't try to demonstrate your intelligence and ability by using an extensive or specialized vocabulary. If your prospect doesn't understand you, he's not going to open up. And even if he does understand you, he's not going to be impressed by a show-off.

- *Keep the tone positive.* Ask questions that allow the prospect to consider solutions and, when appropriate, express agreement with what you've said. Don't criticize other vendors.

- *Ask your question and be quiet.* Don't be afraid of silence; give your prospect time to answer you.

Wants and Needs

In Strategy Four, we talked about the difference between wants and needs and explained that people buy what they need from people who understand what they want. Here's a story that William T. Brooks and Tom Travisano told in their book, *You're Working Too Hard to Make the Sale!* (McGraw-Hill, 1995), that illustrates this point perfectly.

The assembly line on which semiconductors are made is called a *fab*, from the word fabrication, and the fab manager is in charge of the process. In the semiconductor industry, the rejection rate for chips is enormous because manufacturing them requires a cleaner environment than a hospital operating room. A speck of dust can instantly turn a chip into dust. A key industry buzz-word is *yield*, which refers to the number of good chips a fab pro-duces. When you're producing millions of chips a year, raising the yield by just 1 or 2 percent translates into a lot of chips—and a lot of money. But because the process is so complicated and involves so many steps, it's almost impossible to isolate the parts of the production process that have the greatest impact on yield. Another challenge the fab manager has to deal with is safety because deadly gases are used in the manufacture of computer chips.

So it would seem that a fab manager has two priorities: yield and safety. But things aren't always as they seem.

Fab managers endure a constant parade of salespeople trying to sell them products that will improve their yield or enhance safety—but neither approach works. The fab managers don't believe anyone really knows how to improve yield, and, while the process is poten-tially dangerous, it hasn't killed anyone yet. The real reason these approaches don't work is because they don't address the fab man-agers' primary want, which is far more important than any need.

One fab manager explained it this way: He said that the biggest nightmare of any fab manager is that some weekend, when he's off and enjoying time with friends and family, one of the tanks in which the gases are stored explodes, people are killed, the groundwater is polluted, everything within ten square blocks looks like the surface of the moon, and the fab manager is being sought after by reporters to explain what happened. Sure, the idea of so much death and devastation bothers them, but their real fear is being on TV. That manager said: "You have to understand. We're fab managers, not 'out front' people. You don't take this job to be in the spotlight. Any time one of us is in the media, it's

because a big disaster happened. We just want to get the job done behind the scenes, without being showered with attention. Salespeople just don't understand that."

So when the fab manager agreed to see a sales rep, he expressed cynical boredom as he waited for her to be shown in. "Here comes another yield and safety pitch," he said. But he was wrong because this sales rep shook his hand, sat down, and calmly said, "I know you're right in the bull's-eye, but there's no reason for you to be there. You should be able to have everything go smoothly and quietly for you." That got his attention. She clearly understood not just what he needed, but what he *wanted*, which was to stay out of the spotlight. And at the end of the sales process, she got a huge order. He loved her product, even though many other salespeople had shown him products with identical features and benefits. The reason he loved her product over the others was that she gave him the opportunity to make a want-based purchase.

It's important to understand that when it comes to the decision-maker's wants, you don't have to perform—you just have to understand and communicate your understanding. But if you don't address the wants first, you'll have almost no chance to address the needs.

The Summary Statement

Once you think you understand what your prospect is looking for, use a summary statement to confirm it. The summary statement is something like this:

> "Based on my understanding of what you've said, you need [then list the top three or four needs and wants that you heard]. Is that correct?"

Or this:

"If I understood you correctly, you're saying that [list items from your notes] would solve your problem. Is that accurate?"

The summary statement does two very important things. First, it confirms your understanding of what the prospect is looking for. You have gotten permission to ask questions and make notes of the answers—you know that and the prospect knows that. The summary statement lets you confirm that you are both on the same page. If the response to the summary statement is agreement, you're ready to move to the next step and show the prospect how your product or service will do what they want.

Second, the summary statement gives you an opportunity to clarify anything if there was a misunderstanding. If the response to your summary statement is no, go back and ask more questions until you understand what the prospect really needs. Once you and your prospect agree that you understand his wants and needs, you're ready to move to the next step.

———— KEY LESSONS ————

✳ The sales interview is the time where you identify the prospect's reason for buying and find out how, what, when, and under what conditions they will buy.

✳ Ask permission to ask questions and make notes of the answers. Don't start asking or writing things down until you have requested and obtained permission. This tells prospects that you respect them and you're not going to do anything without them knowing and agreeing to it.

✳ Incorporate a bonding statement that shows you understand your prospect and their business with your statement of intention and permission request.

✳ If you determine that your product or service isn't a true fit for the prospect's wants and needs, be honest and say so.

✳ Give prospects your undivided attention. Listen with your eyes, ears, heart, and soul.

✳ The two types of questions are open-ended and closed-ended. Open-ended questions typically begin with *how, what, who, when,* and *where,* and encourage the prospect to talk at length. Closed-ended questions typically begin with *do, is, are,* and *would,* and require a simple "yes" or "no" answer.

✳ The ability to ask good questions is essential to a successful sales process.

✳ Good questions may *sound* spontaneous, but they are not. Know exactly what you plan to ask before you meet with the prospect. Write your questions down, and refer to them during your conversation.

✳ When it comes to the decision-maker's wants, you don't have to perform, you just have to understand and communicate that understanding.

✳ Once you think you understand what your prospect is looking for, use a summary statement to confirm it. If the prospect indicates that you did not understand, go back to asking questions. If the prospect agrees that you do understand, move to the next step.

Provide the Solution

The next step in the IMPACT system is *apply*—that is, demonstrating the application of your solution. In a traditional selling situation, this would be the presentation; however, we recommend a more customer-focused approach. Get your prospects involved in the process and show them how your product or service can be applied to meet their needs or solve their problems. This is where your own product knowledge is critical, but what really counts is not how much you know about your product or service; it's how good you are at accessing that information and putting it in terms that are meaningful to your prospects.

In the apply step, you will actually repeat back to prospects what they told you was important to them in the probe step. This lets them know you understood what they said, you made notes of what is important to them, and you're going to focus on that when you discuss the solution you're offering. If in the probe step you uncovered three to five dominant needs, wants, or desires, you are going to emphasize those chief dominant issues and *nothing else.* Don't tell them about a fabulous feature that they have no interest in—no matter how great you think it is, or even how great some of your other customers think it is. When you make that mistake, you kill the trust you have worked so hard to build. Remember, it may take ten acts to build trust, but only one to destroy it.

Many years ago, the late Bill Brooks, founder of The Brooks Group, wanted to buy a Volvo station wagon for his wife, Nancy. Because he understood so much about the process and psychology of sales, Bill was one of the easiest customers to sell to. He put everything on the table and if you could meet his needs, you got the sale—you didn't have to work very hard for it. So he went into the Volvo dealership in Greensboro with a 5"x7" card on which he had written everything he and Nancy wanted—the model, color, and specific options. He met the salesperson on the showroom floor, said, "I want to buy this car for my wife," and handed the salesperson the card with all the information. It could have been the easiest sale that salesperson ever made. But instead of letting Bill buy what he wanted, the salesperson glanced at the card Bill gave him, put it in his pocket, and said, "Let me show you this sedan." And that immediately destroyed any trust Bill might have had or been able to develop in the salesperson.

Nancy didn't want a sedan; she wanted a station wagon. And Bill wanted to give Nancy what she wanted, but he didn't want to have to struggle to make the purchase, and he didn't want to have to waste time looking at cars they didn't want. So he politely asked the salesperson to return the card that had the information about what he wanted and said, "Obviously, you don't understand what I was looking for." He walked out and started to drive home. On the way, he passed the Infiniti dealership, stopped, showed the salesperson the card with the details of what he was looking for, and bought an Infiniti that fit the description.

Now, it's entirely possible that the Volvo dealership didn't have the model Bill wanted in stock. If that was the case, though, the salesperson should have been honest. We also know that in many industries salespeople are encouraged to push certain products through the use of spiffs (an immediate, special bonus for the sale of a particular item), and it's possible the Volvo dealership had a spiff on the sedans, and the salesperson figured he had nothing to lose by getting Bill to at least look at the sedan before showing him a station wagon. But the reality is that he lost Bill's trust, respect—and the sale.

The lesson here is let your customers buy what they want; it's much easier than trying to sell them something they don't want.

Say What Needs to be Said—Then Stop Talking

A common mistake well-intended salespeople make is that they talk too much about things that don't matter to their prospects. The only thing you need to talk about is what your prospects say is important to them. If they want more information, they'll let you know. You can find out by asking feedback questions when you make your recommendations. Here's how that conversation might look:

> *You:* "Sam, you indicated to me that you are looking for security, timely delivery, and a warranty. Is that correct?"

> *Prospect:* "Yes."

The only thing the prospect can say at this point is yes because you made notes. And you might think that the safety feature of your product is great, but it's not important to your prospect, so don't bring it up. If you do, you may as well say, "I wasn't listening and I don't care what you want, I'm only interested in selling you what I have."

You: "Great. I want to make sure that I am clear on what you are trying to accomplish. On-time delivery, warranty, and security—which of those is most important to you?"

Prospect: "Security."

You: "Security, good. Security is number one to you. What would be number two?"

Prospect: "Timely delivery."

You: "So it's security, timely delivery, and warranty in that order. Is that accurate?"

Prospect: "Yes."

You: "Good. Based on what you've said to me regarding security, I'm going to recommend our [name of product] because [explain why you are making the recommendation]. How does that sound?"

Prospect: "Good."

You: "Excellent. You indicated your number two priority is timely delivery. Based on that, I'm going to recommend [whatever will meet that need]. Does that sound like what you were trying to accomplish?"

Prospect: "Yes."

You: "Great. Now, your third priority is warranty, which is why I'm recommending [add details]. Can you see how that would work for you?"

> *"You don't get paid for the hour. You get paid for the value you bring to the hour."*
>
> —Jim Rohn

What you're doing with this approach is asking feedback questions with each recommendation to make sure that you and the prospect are in agreement on the solutions you're

presenting. This works only when the solutions you're offering are actually based on the wants and needs the prospect has expressed. Put your solution—your presentation—in terms of what's important to your prospect, and don't waste their time on things they don't care about, no matter how important you think those things might be.

Show Them the Money

Even if you didn't see *Jerry McGuire*, you've probably seen a clip from that movie of Tom Cruise screaming, "Show me the money!" What this cliché has come to mean is that if you're negotiating a deal, you need to put something out there that proves you are really interested and ready to commit, that you're not just talking.

In a sales situation, certainly it's the customer who is going to eventually have to spend the money, but it's the salesperson who must "show them the money (the value)" during the sales process. That means demonstrating clearly how your product or service will meet the prospect's needs and getting the prospect involved from the start.

To your prospects, any price is too high until they understand the value of the application of the product or service to solve their problem or fill their particular need. That's why you need to make the correct recommendation in such a way that your prospects see, feel, and experience the application of the product or service to solve their problems, resolve their issues, or fill their specific needs. When

> *"Practice isn't the thing you do once you're good. It's the thing you do that makes you good."*
> —Malcolm Gladwell

you do, the transfer of ownership—the sale—will begin to take place and price objections will fade. This transfer of ownership process must first occur in the prospect's mind before it can occur tangibly in a sale, which is why you want to put your prospects in the position of ownership as early as possible in the process.

Application-Based vs. Demonstration-Based Selling

The term "sales presentation" is not truly applicable to today's dynamic sales environments. It implies a one-way transfer of information that results in the completion of a purchase. But many salespeople still think all they need to do to make a sale is to have a good sales presentation—that is, simply show a prospect how your product or service works. But if you want people to buy when you're finished, that's not enough.

There are two basic types of sales approaches: application-based and demonstration-based. Application-based selling allows you to create value, stack benefits, reduce perceived emotional costs, and make a presentation that is 100 percent on target to address your prospect's most pressing needs or situations. This approach builds value around your recommendation by allowing prospects to emotionally involve themselves in the process and see themselves using what you are recommending. They can experience how the application of your solution will fulfill what they are trying to accomplish.

Demonstration-based selling is inflexible and leads to nothing but price problems and feature/function-loaded standard presentations. With this style of selling, all you're doing is saying, "Here's what this does, and it may or may not have any significance or meaning to you." Often the demonstration includes giving the prospect a chance to try the product.

This type of presentation frequently leads to what is known as the puppy dog close, named for the idea that if you show someone a cute, cuddly puppy, let him hold and play with the puppy and take it home for a weekend, he'll keep it, even though he rationally knows that he doesn't want or need it. The salesperson doesn't sell the puppy; the puppy does the selling. The salesperson gives a demonstration, and while the prospect is trying to politely escape without making a commitment because he has failed to see the value in the product, the salesperson says, "Take it home for the weekend and see how you like it," or "You don't need to make a decision today. I know your [spouse, boss, kids, associates, whatever] hasn't seen this yet. The best thing to do is let them discover the great benefits for themselves. Why don't you just take [the product] home [or to the office] for a day or two so they can try it out and you can get their opinion? We'll get together in a couple of days to talk about their experiences and wrap this up. Does that sound fair?" Most people never bring whatever it is back, they buy it. This is, by the way, a very common strategy used in automobile sales.

The problem with this sales approach is that it has no regard for what the prospect really wants and needs. It's simply the salesperson giving the prospect something because he is trying to make a sale. He doesn't care whether the prospect truly likes it or not, or wants it or not; he just wants the prospect to take it because he knows that if he can do that, he can probably close the deal. This might work on a prospect once, but it's not the basis for a long-term, mutually beneficial relationship that is customer-focused and likely to result in strong referrals.

By contrast, application-based selling lets you honestly say, "Susan, I want to show you how my solution provides what you are looking to accomplish. This is how it does that." Then, during your presentation, you ask feedback questions, such as:

"What do you think about what we have discussed?"
"How do you feel about this?"
"Does this look like something that's going to work for you?"
"What do you like about what we have discussed so far?"

> "Formulate and stamp indelibly on your mind a mental picture of yourself as succeeding. Hold this picture tenaciously. Never permit it to fade. Your mind will seek to develop the picture. Do not build up obstacles in your imagination."
>
> —Norman Vincent Peale

This lets you know that you and the prospect are still together as you move through the apply step. Any time the prospect indicates that you are not together, you can move back to the probe step, asking questions, such as "What makes you say that?" or "Why do you feel that way?" That lets you figure out where you lost the connection and what you have to do to get it back. It keeps the prospect comfortably involved because you're not trying to sell something; you're engaging in a dialogue about possible solutions.

Make sure your feedback questions are legitimate and offer the prospect a chance to respond honestly and completely. There

The Value of Product Knowledge

Real product knowledge—the kind that has value in a sales situation—is not how much you know about your product or service; it's how good you are at accessing that information and putting it in terms that are meaningful to your prospect.

The average sales presentation consists of six to eight features or benefits. After 24 hours, the average prospect remembers only one of these, and in 39 percent of cases, they remember that one incorrectly; in 49 percent of cases, they remember something that wasn't brought up at all. When you can put your product's features and benefits in terms that your prospects can relate to, prospects are more likely to remember them accurately.

is a long-time sales closing technique that consists of asking the prospect a series of questions that are hard to answer with anything other than a "yes" so that you get him into the habit of saying yes, and the close is theoretically automatic. The problem with that close is that many salespeople use insulting, no-brainer questions (such as "You want to save money, don't you?" or "You want your family to be safe, don't you?"), and prospects can easily spot the technique. Make your questions genuine. Let prospects know you're sincerely interested in their feedback, and your questions are as much for their benefit as your own.

When You Get to the Money Part

In every sale, you eventually get to the part where you have to talk about price. It's more than likely going to happen when you're asking feedback questions, and the prospect will answer you with something like, "This sounds good. What's it going to cost me?"

A high percentage of your prospects have likely already shopped the internet, and they have a pretty good idea of what the pricing is, or at least the range they can expect. When you answer the price question, never just state the price alone. Say something like "The price is $XXX, and that includes this, this, and this. It also includes that, that, and that." That's known as stacking the benefits on your price. If you just say the price without stacking the benefits, whatever the price is will almost always be too high. When you just toss out a number, the prospect has nothing to compare it with and can't identify exactly what he's getting, so the perception will likely be: "Whatever it is, it's too much."

It's easy to make fun of the "but wait, there's more" line you see in most infomercials, but it's done over and over because it works. The infomercial copywriters stack the benefits twice: First, before giving the price, the announcer summarizes the benefits ("It does this and this, and all these things, for the low price of

$XX.") and then stacks the benefits again with the "buy now" offer ("But wait, there's more! If you call now, you'll get this and that, absolutely free, just pay the shipping and handling.").

Salespeople often panic when asked about price because they're afraid it's going to introduce a negative into the situation. They fear that the price is going to be perceived as too high, and they're going to get some pushback about it. Well, if you haven't built sufficient value in your presentation, that's exactly what's going to happen. But if you have been customer-focused and you've demonstrated how your product will meet the prospect's needs, the price will be just one more product-related question for you to answer. And remember, people can't buy something if they don't know how much it's going to cost.

> *"Three things that never come back: the spent arrow; the spoken word; the lost opportunity."*
> —William George Plunkett

With that said, let's also stress this: Never give the price prematurely, quote a price to an unsold buyer, or present your price until you have had the opportunity to build sufficient value around it.

When prospects bring up price too early in the process, postpone responding for as long as you can. The easiest way to do that is to say, "Before I tell you the price, may I tell you about what the price is going to include?" Then you can return to building value in your product by talking about how the product will meet the prospect's needs.

What Not to Do When Discussing Price

Never put a modifier on your price, such as "Our regular/standard price is . . ." or "Our retail price is . . ." Every modifier on the word "price" invites another price question and negotiation. So if you say, "Our regular price is . . ." you could get a response such as "That's great, but what's my price?" or even "What's your irregular price?"

You may have seen salespeople say something like this when asked about price: "Our regular price is $89.95, but for you it's going to be different. If you'll allow me a few minutes to go over some additional issues, I'll explain your price."

The problem with that is that even if the price you have in mind for that particular prospect is discounted from the "regular" price of $89.95, they're going to want it still lower. They're going to try to talk you down from whatever you end up quoting because you've just told them that you're willing to negotiate. You've started a cycle where the prospect feels he can talk you down and get a better price than whatever you quote.

This can happen even with prospects who don't mind paying more for something if they believe it has value and will perform as promised—but even those prospects don't want to be the only person paying top dollar. They know that if they don't ask, the answer is always no. We all want to feel like we are shrewd negotiators, even when we've made the decision to buy no matter what the price. Think about this: How often have you asked for a better price and not gotten it but still made the purchase because you wanted the product and you felt like the original price was worth it? You will have customers who do the same thing.

Another way you set yourself up for failure is when you use statements like "We really want your business, so . . ." and "Tell me where we need to be . . ." This is devaluing your product and makes you appear desperate, and it generally results in an unprofitable sale or even no sale.

How to Present Your Price

When it's time to present the price, connect the value of your product to the price. As we've already said, stack the benefits to create added value and price acceptance. Stand firm on your price because it's worth it.

If the prospect wants to negotiate, never just drop the price. Take away something that reduces the value along with the price. For example, say something like "If we don't include this [it could be delivery, assembly, or even accessories], we can reduce the price to $XX."

Be prepared for savvy purchasers to look for other points to negotiate beyond the basic price, such as payment terms or delivery schedules. They might, for example, want longer to pay, or they might be willing to make a purchase commitment at a level that will qualify them for a quantity discount if you will agree to make smaller quantity deliveries over a period of time. Know what you can offer in these areas so you can respond to the requests on the spot.

Avoid Comparisons

Don't let your product or service become a commodity. A commodity is any product for which there is intense competition and no discernable differentiation in the marketplace. Even if you have strong competition, figure out a way to set yourself apart. The difference may be in the product, or in the support you offer, or it might be your own individual knowledge or expertise—all those issues add value and remove your product from the commodity category.

If a prospect tries to push you into the commodity category with statements such as "You want to charge X, but I can get the same thing for Y [less] at another company. Will you match or beat their price?" say "No. The solution I'm offering is not the same thing. Yes, my price is higher, but are you expecting to get my expertise for their price? That's unrealistic. Would you do that with your product?" Sometimes that works, sometimes it doesn't—but if it doesn't, you shouldn't care because you weren't going to make the sale to a prospect with that mind-set anyway. Another approach to prospects who are trying to treat your product as a commodity is, when they say they can get what you have to offer elsewhere for less, ask this: "I understand that you've probably gotten prices that are less. Let me ask you this: Why are you still talking to me?"

Never allow your prospects to compare apples to apples. Make them compare apples to pears. You don't want to be just another apple in a bushel of apples. Separate your offering from every competitor's offering so it's impossible to compare apples to apples.

> *"Opportunities are never lost. The other fellow takes those you miss."*
> —Unknown

Finally, never let your product or service be compared item-for-item, benefit-by-benefit or feature-by-feature to any other competitive product. You must sell any benefit of your product as if it is an exclusive.

Dealing with Price Objections

No matter how much product value you build into your presentation, you will occasionally get price objections. In one way or another, the prospect will tell you that your price is too high.

One way to deal with a price objection is to acknowledge what the prospect has said with a noncommittal response, such as "Oh?" "Hmmm" or "Really?" Then wait for a response—let them tell you why they feel that way. Once they do, you have the opportunity to resell.

Another approach is to justify your price. Say something like "Our price is high, I suppose. It's higher than most because it includes more than most, and that's what makes it worth the price we charge. Here's what it actually includes . . ." and then list the value items the prospect has indicated are important. More simply, try this: "You know, you are right. We are not cheap. That's exactly why you should be doing business with us." Or even this: "We're not cheap. Are you?" Then see what kind of response you get. You might be surprised.

Some prospects will border on offensive when expressing a price objection, saying things like "That's outrageous," or "I'm not paying that." To statements such as the first one, simply say, "Why do you say that?" and wait for an answer. To statements such as the second, try this: "I understand. That's interesting. I have many clients who pay that every day, and they are very happy. What upsets you about the price?"

Deal with price objections head-on. Some people may perceive that as arrogant, but you shouldn't care. If they are price buyers, they're not your customers anyway because you don't sell on price; you sell on value.

——— KEY LESSONS ———

⁎ Get your prospects involved in the process as you show them how your product or service can be applied to meet their needs or solve their problems.

⁎ Remember that what counts is not how much you know about your product or service; it's how good you are at accessing what you know and putting those things in terms that are meaningful to your prospects.

⁎ Before you present your solution, repeat back to prospects what they told you was important to them. This lets them know you understood what they said, made notes of what is important to them, and you're going to focus on that when you discuss what you're offering.

⁎ Let your customers buy what they want; it's much easier than trying to sell them something they don't want.

⁎ As you make your recommendations, ask feedback questions to make sure you're focusing on what's important to your prospects and that you're providing sufficient information.

Any time the prospect indicates that you are not together, move back to the probe step and ask questions that will let you figure out where you lost connection and how to get it back. Be sure your feedback questions are legitimate, and offer the prospect a chance to respond honestly and completely.

* Put your solution in terms of what's important to your prospects, and don't waste their time on things they don't care about.

* Get prospects involved in the solution so they can see it working for them. This allows the transfer of ownership—the sale— to begin to take place. The transfer of ownership must first occur in the prospect's mind before it can occur as a tangible sale.

* The two basic types of sales approaches are application-based and demonstration-based. Application-based selling allows you to create value, stack benefits, reduce perceived emotional costs, and make a presentation that is 100 percent on target to address your prospect's most pressing needs. Demonstration-based selling is inflexible and leads to nothing but price problems and feature/function-loaded standard presentations.

* When you give the price, never just state the price alone; always stack the benefits on your price. Never put a modifier on the price, or offer to negotiate. Be ready to justify your price with value statements.

* If the prospect wants to negotiate, never just drop the price. Take away something that reduces the value along with the price.

* Don't be afraid of answering the price question. When you have been customer-focused and demonstrated how your

product will meet the prospect's wants and needs, the price will be just one more product-related question for you to answer.

* Don't allow your product or service to become a commodity, which is any product for which there is intense competition and no discernable differentiation in the marketplace.

Provide the Proof

The fifth step of the IMPACT process is *convince,* and you do that by offering proof of your claims in ways that increase the trust the prospect has in you, demonstrate the value of the purchase, and validate the wisdom of your prospect's buying decision.

What drives the importance of the convince step is that when people believe strongly enough, they act. Prospects expect the salesperson to make claims about their product or service. While they may not distrust the salesperson, they may not strongly believe the product claims he makes, either. What is more impressive to prospects is when someone else makes positive claims about a product or service.

Before people will buy anything, they must believe what they hear and feel about that product or service. That's why you must offer a third-party validation or social proof that you can in fact

> "Be creative. Use unconventional thinking. And have the guts to carry it out."
>
> —Lee Iaccoca

provide what you have recommended. The reasoning behind this strategy is simple: How many times have you made a major purchase, but before you did, you asked friends or people you trusted for their opinion or advice? That's the main driver behind the success of consumer sites such as Angie's List; people want trusted sources of information before they buy.

What Is Your Refund or Return Policy?

Consider these two statements:

1. All sales final.

2. Satisfaction guaranteed or your money will be cheerfully refunded.

Which is likely to give you greater confidence when making a purchase decision?

Part of the convince step should include a discussion of your performance guarantees along with your refund and return policy. Of course, you want to focus on why your prospects will be completely satisfied with your product or service, but you should also give them the extra security of letting them know what will happen if they're not.

A customer-focused refund and return policy clearly states the conditions under which a customer can return a product (or stop using a service) and qualify for a refund and what the respective obligations of both the customer and the company are. Don't make your customers jump through unnecessary or complicated hoops to get their money back if they are not satisfied with your product. On the other hand, it's perfectly acceptable to set reasonable parameters, such as time limits, documentation, and other conditions, for issuing refunds.

The same dynamic is at work when you provide proof of your claims in a sales situation.

People are also impressed when they have the opportunity to experience the claims and enjoy the successes promised to them. After that happens, they are often willing to provide a testimonial for you and become part of the proof you offer other prospects.

This step of the process is important for four key reasons. First, it makes your prospects aware of their own concept of value and how well you have satisfied it. Second, it shows your prospects how great the benefits of ownership will make them feel. Third, it helps your prospects gradually experience what ownership will be like. And fourth, it validates the wisdom of your prospect's choice from a value perspective.

How Do You Prove Your Claims?

There are a number of ways you can prove your claims, and not all are appropriate for every product or service. It's a good idea to have two or more proof methods to use. Some suggestions:

- *Demonstrations.* Show prospects how your product works. For vehicles, you take the prospects on a test drive. For equipment, you show it in operation. The demonstration needs to be conducted by someone with some skill in operating the product so that it's shown in its best light. If it's not possible to do an on-site demonstration, you can show a video—although the impact won't be as strong.
- *Trial tests.* In some ways, this is akin to the puppy dog close we discussed in Strategy Eight. Let people use the product in some way on a trial basis to see how it performs in their environment. This is effective for many types of heavy machinery, office equipment, and other items that can be temporarily used. The key to a successful trial test is to clearly define the trial period, the parameters of the test,

and the mutual expectations. For example, you may need to restrict the individuals at your prospect's company who can use the equipment, perhaps because it requires special training or there are liability issues.

The difference between a trial test and the puppy dog close is that with the puppy dog close, you are expecting the product to sell itself. With a trial test, you have already done the selling and are simply using the trial to prove your claims.

· *Customer testimonials.* One of the most effective proof methods is testimonials from loyal customers. You may present them in a list of short comments or in letters of recommendation. You can include testimonials in your printed marketing materials, on your website, or in a separate proof book that you show to prospects. You may or may not choose to reveal the full identity of the individual offering the testimonial, depending on the nature of the product and industry. However, if you choose to keep certain details confidential, be sure you have complete back-up data on file so that you can verify the testimonial if necessary.

When you ask for a testimonial, find out if the customer is willing to also be a reference and would accept calls from prospects who want to know more about his experience with you and your product. In some cases, you may even want to be able to take a prospect on a visit to an existing customer's location to show your product in operation and allow the prospect to talk to the customer directly.

· *Third-party endorsements.* This type of endorsement typically comes from celebrities or established authorities in your field—individuals who may or may not be your customers. How effective they are will depend on the nature of the industry and the credibility of the endorser. Keep in mind that celebrity endorsements can be quite risky. When a celebrity is on top, you have the benefit of his popularity; if he falls from grace and his reputation suffers, the value of the endorsement plummets as well. There is also the question, which was discussed in detail in *Flashpoint: Seven Core Strategies for Rapid-Fire Business Growth*, of whether a celebrity endorsement really increases the perceived value of your product or simply promotes the celebrity.

Another type of third-party endorsement is positive comments posted on independent consumer sites, such as the previously mentioned Angie's List, ConsumerSearch.com, Epinions.com, and so on. Periodically do an internet search on your product and company name to see what people are saying about you and decide if you can use that information to prove your product claims.

· *Independent testing and research.* There are a number of independent testing and research operations that can validate your claims. For example, Underwriters Laboratories (UL) is an independent product safety certification organization that has been testing products and writing safety standards for more than a century. J.D. Power and Associates conducts independent and unbiased surveys of customer satisfaction, product quality, and buyer behavior. Most industries have some type of independent testing and research organization that is recognized and respected.

· *Journal articles.* Positive mentions of your company and product in professional journals can support your product performance claims as well as enhance your company's position in the market.

> *"Depend on the rabbit's foot if you will, but remember it didn't work for the rabbit."*
> —R.E. Shay

These are just a few ideas for how you can convince a prospect that the solution you are recommending will indeed work. The key thing to remember about this strategy is that if you make a claim for your product or service, you should be able to prove it. In fact, if you can't validate something, don't mention it.

KEY LESSONS

✳ Before someone will buy, he must believe what he hears and feels about the product or service.

✳ Providing the proof that will convince your prospects of the value of your product does four things: It makes your prospects aware of their concept of value and how well you have satisfied it, it shows them how great they will feel when they own your product or service, it helps them experience what ownership will be like, and it validates the wisdom of their choice from a value perspective.

✳ Prove your claims with demonstrations, trial tests, customer testimonials, third-party endorsements, independent testing and research, and journal articles.

✳ Have a clear, customer-focused refund and return policy that will give your customers confidence in their purchase decision.

✳ Be able to prove every claim you make about your product or service; if you can't prove something, don't bring it up.

Seal the Deal

The final step of the IMPACT process is to *tie it up*—that is, ask the prospect to buy, negotiate the agreement, and cement the sale. While some sales training programs focus heavily on this part of the sales process, relying a great deal on manipulative closing techniques, we take a different approach. Finalizing agreements and closing sales are not stand-alone events; they are a natural consequence of what has happened earlier in the process. It is *not* some huge crescendo that you should build toward.

Though the close is a natural part of doing the first five steps of the IMPACT system well, there is one thing you still must do: You must ask the prospect to buy. The decision to purchase is theirs to make, not yours to assume. So you must ask for their commitment.

It's amazing that approximately 65 percent of all salespeople fail to ask for the sale—often even when the prospect is giving buying signals. A woman we know recalls the time an encyclopedia salesperson knocked on her door. This was many years ago, before personal computers and the internet, and she thought it would be convenient to have a good set of reference books at home. Our friend had spent a summer selling encyclopedias herself, and she was at the time working in sales, so she had some empathy for the salesperson. As he went through his presentation, she answered all of his feedback questions honestly. She agreed that the books were clearly of a high quality and although she didn't have children, she indicated that she would use them and could afford them—even talked about how they would save her from having to drive to the library. Then the salesperson moved to the bonus portion of his presentation, the "buy now and you'll get this for free" segment (equivalent to the "but wait!" line in today's infomercials).

"The bonus items were some cookbooks and a set of children's storybooks, so when he asked if I would use them, I said no. I didn't cook, and I didn't have children," she told us. "But I had said that I would use the encyclopedias, that I thought they were a good value, and I had responded enthusiastically to all of his 'trial close' questions about those books. I was waiting for him to ask for the order, and I would have signed the contract and written him a check. So I was surprised when, after I told him I wouldn't use the bonus items, he just packed up his stuff and left—and he walked out without a sale he would have gotten if he had just asked for it." This salesperson had obviously been taught that the bonus items would clinch the sale and that's when he should bring out the contract and close. When he found a prospect that didn't fit the mold he had been trained to sell to—when, as we say, he was using a script but his prospect didn't know the lines—he dropped the ball and missed a sale. The moral of this story is always ask for the order. Never walk away from a sales call without asking for the business.

Let's digress for a moment and clarify what we mean by asking for the order or the business. Depending on your product or industry, the "order" might not be the final sale. It might be the next step in the process. Many products and services take multiple sales calls to close. So, for example, the "order" might be an agreement to a trial installation of equipment. It might be that you've passed the first round of screening and can move on to presenting your product to the next level of decision-maker. It might be just a commitment on the part of the prospect about when a decision will be made. You should go into every sales call knowing what you want the outcome to be, and asking for the order means asking for that outcome.

While it's important to ask for the sale, it's also important to never ask for the sale until you are reasonably sure you are going to be successful with it—and you are going to be successful with it if you have built sufficient value, allowed the prospect to engage in dialogue, asked feedback questions to make sure you are on the same page, confirmed that you are providing the value the prospect is looking for, reached price agreement, and agreed on delivery terms. If you and the prospect are together on everything, there is no reason why he shouldn't buy.

When you get to that point and the prospect says no, there are only three reasons why:

1. The prospect was misleading you. Sometimes that happens. With experience, you'll learn to spot it early.
2. The prospect had a change of heart because the trust went away at some point. That means you missed something—that you didn't stay in sync with the prospect.

> *"People who produce good results feel good about themselves."*
> —Ken Blanchard

3. The prospect does not have the authority or capacity to make the purchase.

The third reason—that the prospect does not have the authority or capacity to buy—should never happen because early in the process you should have asked qualifying questions to establish this issue. If you did that and the prospect indicated at the time that he could make the decision, then later on says he can't, he has either lied to you or has lost trust in you and is looking for a non-confrontational way out.

In a perfect world, these situations shouldn't occur. In the real world, of course, they do—no matter how professional and thorough

A Stall or a Legitimate Objection?

Learn to recognize the difference between a stall and a legitimate objection. A stall is an attempt to slow the sales process, such as "Let me think about it." People will stall when they are uncertain and uneasy, or when they have lost trust in you or your product. They stall when something has caused them to have second thoughts. Sometimes a prospect will stall when he is not the actual decision-maker, doesn't have the authority to buy, or is in some other way not truly a qualified prospect. When prospects stall, you need to gently draw them out to figure out what has happened and get them moving forward again.

A legitimate objection is when your prospect seeks an answer to a genuine concern that hasn't yet been answered to his satisfaction. This can happen at the end of a sales presentation if the prospect remembers something important that he had forgotten about. With a legitimate objection, the prospect is clearly telling you that he's not saying no, but he needs more information or has an issue that has to be resolved before the sale can be finalized.

you are. Prospects will sometimes say no. Sometimes they will just prefer another product or service over yours—not because there is anything wrong with yours, but they just like the other better. But if you are professional, thorough, and using a customer-focused sales system, your success rate will skyrocket, and the occasional lost sale will be insignificant.

Eight Ways to Make Closing Easy

Two things happen when you fail to ask someone to buy your product or service: 1) You don't get the sale, and 2) they buy from someone else, don't buy at all, or defer their decision. When you don't ask for the order, you haven't finished your job. It's like a hair stylist who only cut half of your hair. Or a mechanic who took a broken part out of your car but didn't put the new one in.

Incorporate these ideas with the strategies that make up the IMPACT system to help you get your transactions finalized:

1. Understand what your real job is. It's not public relations, customer service, technical support or anything else. It's making sales. Period.

2. Learn how to use feedback questions ("How does this look?" "Would this work for you?") to be sure you're on target with your presentations.

3. Learn how to listen and observe better. Listen to what prospects say. Better yet, listen to what they really mean. Be sensitive to non-verbal behavior.

4. Master the art of value-added selling so you can provide your product or service in a way that makes it virtually irresistible.

> "It's not the employer who pays the wages. Employers only handle the money. It's the customer who pays the wages."
>
> —Henry Ford

When to Ask for Referrals

You have probably had the experience as a customer of being asked for referrals immediately after making the purchase but before you've had a chance to actually use the product. If you felt uncomfortable giving referrals under those circumstances, you're not alone. We recommend that you never ask for referrals immediately after any sale. Ask only after you have earned the right to do so by delivering a quality product and/or service. Besides, the referrals will be of a higher quality when your customer has had time to think about who to recommend you to. And, if you ask for a referral and the customer indicates that there's a problem, you have a chance to correct it and restore your relationship.

5. Be sure you're in front of qualified buyers who really do have the authority to say yes and make the purchase.

6. Believe in yourself, your sales process, organization, and product or service so much that you want others to become a part of it—and ask them to do so by purchasing. Show your passion.

7. Learn, apply, and master nonmanipulative, well-applied, non-heavy-handed ways to finalize a transaction, and use them consistently. Old-school, memorized closes are dead; they don't work, so don't use them.

8. Learn the fundamentals of negotiation and how to ask people to buy after agreeing on terms.

The Best Way to Close

If you've had any sales training at all, you're probably familiar with a variety of closing techniques. We've already talked about the puppy dog close, which is when you allow the prospect to take possession of the product in the hopes that he won't want to bring it back.

Another popular closing technique is the take-away close, which plays on the natural human tendency to want what we can't have. The salesperson will say things like, "This isn't for everyone," or "Only a few people appreciate the quality of this," or even, "I'm not sure if you will qualify for this." There's the order form close, where the salesperson puts the order form or contract in front of the prospect, asks him to fill in part of the information, and says that he (the salesperson) will do the rest. And there's the either/or close, where the salesperson gives the prospect a choice, such as "Would you like the basic package, or would the premium package be a better fit for you?" We could go on for pages on techniques like these, but suffice it to say that if you recognize even some of them, chances are your prospects will as well. And more important is that these methods are manipulative. The true top performing salespeople don't have to resort to tricks to close deals. If you need techniques such as these to close a sale, you haven't done a particularly good job of selling.

Finalizing transactions is not a function of how many ways to close a sale the salesperson can memorize. Instead, it is learning one single method and mastering it. If you have been using feedback questions as you learned in Strategy Eight, your prospect's answers should have been telling you how they think and indicating their readiness to buy. And when they are ready to buy, you close. It's really as simple as that.

The Assumptive Close

The assumptive close assumes the sale and can be in the form of a question or a statement. It's doing everything right, getting the feedback you need, maintaining a positive attitude, believing that you are going to be successful, and then saying something that will allow you to tie it up. You might say, "Let's get the order in process so you can have the product as soon as possible," or "Shall we go ahead and take care of the paperwork?" or something similar.

Use the System to Learn the System

Another way to make IMPACT work for you is to use the system to learn the system. Here's how:

- Investigate your own selling situation to determine what you need to do to become more effective at selling your products to your market.
- Meet the system by learning the six basic steps.
- Probe into the system to study all the tools it gives you.
- Apply each of those tools to your own selling needs.
- Convince yourself that the system really works with whatever you are selling.
- Tie it up and take it home by putting what you've learned into practice.

Again, don't say this until you feel sure that the prospect is ready to buy. In most cases, your intuition will be on target. By the way, the assumptive close is the only close that is statistically successful.

Pulling It All Together

At The Brooks Group, we practice what we preach. Here's how one of our own account managers used the IMPACT system to close a substantial deal.

The client, a *Fortune 500* firm, manufactures and sells automobile paint and is a vendor to vehicle manufacturers. They had been doing business with another sales training company and had a good relationship with them for years. But the client decided they needed a customized training program, which the other company could not provide, so they started shopping.

During the investigation step, we identified the key people (internal advocate, check writer, decision-maker, and user). The decision-maker was actually a committee, not an individual. Our

internal advocate told us some crucial information. He let us know that the problem was big, that solving it was a high priority for the decision-makers, and that there was no company other than ours that could provide the solution they needed. As we went through the probe step with the decision-makers, we were able to confirm what our internal advocate had told us. When we moved to the apply step and showed the client what we could do, we quoted a fee that was 20 percent higher than what they were paying. The decision-makers said the price was out of line.

Because we had been thorough during the investigation step and we knew what their situation was, we didn't budge on the price. Instead, we asked questions designed to help them realize that we were the only firm that could provide the solution they needed. That conversation went from "You're crazy if you think we're going to pay this price!" to "If we are going to pay this price, here's what we expect." The expectations were reasonable and we were comfortable committing to them.

At the tie it up step, the client made a six-year commitment to our program—but we wouldn't have gotten there had we not carefully and strategically followed all the steps of the IMPACT system.

It's Not the Color of the Bow, It's the Quality of the Knot

When you tie it up, you shouldn't need to do anything spectacular or flashy. You simply watch for buying signals—that is, things the prospect will say or do that indicate he has all the information he needs and is ready to close the deal—and then you ask for the sale. When the prospect says yes, you do the paperwork or whatever else is necessary to finish the transaction. This isn't some spectacular, awe-inspiring part of the process; it's the natural evolution of everything you did up to this point. Give yourself a pat on the back and move on to the next opportunity.

KEY LESSONS

* Finalizing agreements and closing sales are not stand-alone events; they are a consequence of what has happened earlier in the process.

* You must ask the prospect to buy. Approximately 65 percent of all salespeople fail to ask for the sale, and that is often the reason they don't make the sale. When you don't ask for the order, you haven't finished your job.

* Never ask for the sale until you are reasonably sure you are going to get it. Work on the various steps of the sales process until you have feedback from the prospect that indicates he is ready to buy.

* Many products and services take multiple sales calls to close. You should go into every sales call knowing what you want the outcome to be, and asking for the order means asking for that outcome.

* Learn to recognize the difference between a stall and a legitimate objection. A stall is an attempt to slow the sales process. A legitimate objection is when the prospect seeks an answer to a genuine concern that hasn't yet been satisfactorily answered.

* The assumptive close assumes the sale and can be in the form of a question or a statement. Do this after you have done everything else right, gotten the feedback you need, maintained a positive attitude, and believe you are going to be successful. Your close does not need to be spectacular or flashy.

* Ask for referrals only after you have earned the right to do so by delivering a quality product and/or service.

part three

Manage Right

High performing salespeople are not easy to manage. In fact, of all the groups of workers, these may be the most challenging for managers. But failure to manage salespeople effectively will almost certainly result in chaos.

Your sales force needs to work together as a team for a common goal, but this can be difficult to pull off because high performers have strong egos. They are independent thinkers who are highly motivated by money, energized by the hunt, and often very entrepreneurial. They don't want to be managed—and they certainly don't want to be micromanaged. They believe in their own ability to get things done, and they think that their numbers and performance speak for themselves, so there should be no discussion. At the same time, if they do well on their own, they will really shine under good management.

The secret to managing a high performing sales team is to do it so your people don't feel like they are being managed. The next five strategies will show you how to do that.

Let the Salespeople Sell and the Managers Manage

In many ways, a strong sales team is similar to a championship sports team—you have an incredible amount of talent that requires strong coaching and effective management to reach its full potential. It's interesting that the best coaches and managers tend to come not from the top talent but from the ranks of the average players—those players who were good enough to make the professional team but who never rose to the status of superstar. They know the game and how to play it well. Their egos are healthy but not monumental. They don't need to always be the center of attention. They don't mind helping someone else shine in the spotlight—in fact, they actually enjoy it. At the same time, they are strong-willed, no-nonsense people who command respect.

That's the kind of person you need as a sales manager. The role of the sales manager is to set the standards for performance and hold

the sales team accountable to those standards. That sounds simple, but it isn't easy.

Most companies operate on the assumption that successful salespeople make successful managers, but this is not the reality. While promoting from within is a good policy, promoting your best salespeople to management positions is rarely the best strategy. Your top performing salesperson is almost never your top performing sales manager. The parameters for success in those two roles in terms of behaviors, values, attitudes, and skills are 180 degrees apart—which is why putting a sales superstar in a sales management position will usually blow up on you. And yet, companies still insist on doing this.

"Be not afraid of greatness."
—William Shakespeare

Another critical mistake we see companies routinely make is that they provide no training or at best minimal training for their sales managers. Even companies that have decent sales training programs for their reps tend to overlook training the managers. When you think about it, that makes absolutely no sense. Why would you put people whose skills don't match the needs of the job into a position, then compound that error by not teaching them how to do the job?

Selling and managing salespeople are two very different roles with different demands and expectations. People need to be trained to handle those different demands and expectations and given the tools to fulfill them.

Setting a Career Path for the Top Performers

If you have top sales performers on your team who are expecting to move into management, you can do them—and your company—a huge favor by redirecting their career expectations. The first step in that process is to help them see how unhappy and frustrated they would be in a sales management position. Sit down and talk with them about how they will like doing the specific things that sales managers must do. Ask questions such as:

- How excited are you about being in the office more than being out in the field? Even though the best sales managers spend a significant amount of time in the field with their salespeople, they're not actually selling and they still have to spend plenty of time in the office dealing with administrative issues.
- How would you like to ride with other salespeople that don't perform as well as you do and help them get better? You can't do the work for them; you have to help them do it themselves.
- How will you like going on sales calls with other salespeople and just observing, not interfering or getting actively involved in the calls?
- How much will you miss having your own territory and customers, and the challenge of the sales process?
- How will you feel if the top performing salespeople earn more than you do? Many companies have commission structures that allow the top performing salespeople to be some of the highest paid people in the organization.

Salespeople who have a strong sense of self-awareness and are honest with themselves will recognize that even though they may have believed that the natural career path for a salesperson is to move into management, they really are better off staying where they are.

After you have this conversation, review their compensation structure. We recommend that your compensation be set up in a way that will allow the top performing salespeople to make more money than their managers. For salespeople who are money-motivated, this

Why Salespeople Leave

It's important to always keep in mind that people don't quit companies; they quit managers. Certainly there are situations where salespeople leave for reasons beyond their control—perhaps a health issue, a spouse being transferred, or other personal reasons—but with rare exceptions, if a member of your sales team is leaving for another job, it's because of a management issue. It's because a manager has created an environment that the salesperson finds so frustrating and even painful to the point that he isn't willing to endure it any longer.

will make the management job less appealing. Even salespeople who are not money-motivated often view income level as a success measurement.

You may want to consider a title of some sort for those top performers that provides some recognition for their achievements. Some will appreciate this; others won't care.

The key thing is to help them change their belief system so they understand that moving into management may not be the best thing for them and that they have the potential to be infinitely more successful and satisfied in a senior sales position.

Selling vs. Nonselling Sales Mangers

There are two types of sales managers: those who sell and those who don't. Selling sales managers have their own territory or a list of accounts for which they are responsible, in addition to their management duties. And just as with salespeople vs. sales managers, this presents a mixture of behavioral, attitudinal, and value requirements that can muddy the water. The sole responsibility of nonselling sales managers is to manage their sales team.

In most cases, nonselling sales managers deliver more value and benefit to the sales team because they can focus on managing and supporting the salespeople without worrying about their own sales quotas. A selling sales manager's loyalties are divided between their own sales responsibilities and supporting their team.

At JK Harris & Company, we learned this lesson the hard way. During a sales team restructuring, we decided to promote our top salespeople to district managers and made them responsible for supervising four sales consultants as well as handling their own territories. We compensated them through an increase in salary plus an override on the performance of the sales consultants they were managing. To say that it didn't work is putting it mildly. It bombed miserably. We made the assumption that our best sales consultants would be the best mentors. We took our top people, assigned three people to each of them for them to mentor, and increased their compensation. The problem was, those top sales consultants wanted to spend their time actually *doing* what they were good at, which was selling, not helping someone else do it. And even the ones who were trying to be good mentors just didn't have the natural skills to do it well. While it might seem logical that the best salesperson would know how to teach someone else how he does it, the reality is that most of them can't. It took us less than three months to recognize our mistake and abandon that structure.

> *"He that would govern others first should be the master of himself."*
> —Philip Massinger

Not all companies have sales teams large enough to support a nonselling manager, but when it's possible, we recommend it.

Recruiting, Selecting, and Training Sales Managers

The tendency for most companies is to move their top salesperson into a sales management role when an opening occurs. There are two basic reasons for this.

One is that it is the nature of top performers, whatever their occupation, to look specifically for a well-defined career path, and they believe incorrectly that a successful sales career path necessitates that they go into sales management. But if you go back to Strategies One and Two, where we talked about hiring the whole person and the assessment process, you'll understand that the characteristics of a top performing sales manager and those of a top performing salesperson are at opposite ends of the spectrum. The nature of a high-performing salesperson is to be on the go constantly, to be engaging, fairly assertive, very independent, and somewhat entrepreneurial in their approach to work. They're focused on completing the sale and moving on to the next prospect. And they're usually lousy teachers and coaches. A strong sales manager, on the other hand, is more concerned about managing the process and helping the salesperson handle the job and stay accountable to the organization. Good sales managers have good teaching and coaching skills.

Unfortunately, we often find that when you have top performing salespeople who believe that sales management is the appropriate next step in their career path and you make them managers, they get into the position and are miserable. They hate it, but they're stuck. And that's when they start looking around for another job because they want to get back into sales, but they don't feel like they can do it without changing companies.

The second reason companies tend to move their top salespeople into sales management roles is that it's easy. That top salesperson is there, you know him, you've known him for years. You trust that he understands you and your culture. Everybody else knows him. On the surface, it looks like the least expensive route to take that will also let you get someone in the role quickly and with minimal effort and hassle. And because he did so well selling for you, it's easy to assume that he'll do well managing. That's a wrong assumption, but, again, it's easy.

We never recommend doing things the hard way when the easy way will work, but this is one time when easy is not the best strategy.

Where to Find Sales Managers

If your sales team is large enough to have multiple sales managers, most often the best practice is to have a combination of those that are brought in from the outside and those that are developed internally.

When you decide to promote a mid-level salesperson to sales manager, you need to make sure that your top performers understand this is not in any way a negative reflection on them or their abilities. If you have applied Strategies Two and Three and have assessments on everyone, you can sit down individually with the top performers and the midlevel person you want to promote and review their profiles. Show them the characteristics revealed by their profiles that indicate their respective suitabilities for the job. Make it clear, especially to the top sales performers, that this isn't about skill and ability, it's about spending your working life doing something you enjoy, that energizes you, something that you find rewarding on multiple levels.

Moving someone from peer to supervisor can be a challenge, especially when you promote a midlevel salesperson to be a manager over high performers. You have to be proactive to avoid a response of "Wait a minute! This person and I used to do the same job, and I do it better, and now I'm going to be reporting to him?!?" It's ideal if the person you promote will not be managing anyone he used to work at the same level with, but that may not always be possible.

If the trust level among your salespeople is high and there is a strong sense of teamwork and camaraderie, it will be easier for you to position the change in a positive way. In any case, you must be absolutely honest with everyone on the sales team and help them

understand the assessment process and why you're taking the action you've decided on.

Once you begin applying the strategies we're presenting, you may actually hire salespeople with the purpose of grooming them to move into management. You can identify these people from their assessments and be candid about your plans for them. Let them—and others on the team as well—know you don't expect them to ever be sales superstars, but at some point, they will take over a management position.

> "Outstanding leaders go out of their way to boost the self-esteem of their personnel. If people believe in themselves, it's amazing what they can accomplish."
>
> —Sam Walton

Companies often resist hiring managers from the outside because those people don't know the company and its culture. Executives and policy-makers figure that it's better to promote from within because of familiarity than to take a chance on an outsider who may not fit. This issue is resolved with a whole person assessment tool such as the TriMetrix we told you about in Strategy Two because that tool will tell you whether or not a salesperson or a sales manager is going to be a fit with your culture. And if you properly use the assessments to evaluate candidates, have benchmarked the position, and hire to the benchmark, you'll likely see significant performance improvements by bringing people in from the outside because, in many cases, it's easier to train them the way you want them from the beginning than it is to untrain and retrain, which is what you have to do when you promote a salesperson to sales manager.

Training Sales Managers

Whether you promote from within or hire from the outside, your sales managers must be trained if they're going to produce the results you want. Yet very few companies—we estimate fewer than

one-fourth—provide their sales managers with any sort of training. They believe the job can be self-taught or that a good salesperson who understands the company's culture will just instinctively know what to do. That's absolutely wrong. Knowing how to manage salespeople is like any other job—you must be taught how to do it. You've got to learn it. And even if you hire a sales manager from another company, chances are excellent that he's never experienced any formal training in how to do the job.

> *"No executive has ever suffered because his subordinates were strong and effective."*
> —Peter Drucker

A strong sales manager can probably teach someone with the right set of basic skills how to be a sales manager. However, the most effective way to train your sales managers is to retain a sales and sales management training firm with a proven track record.

Key Sales Management Functions

You can't manage a sales team from behind a desk. You have to go out and be with your salespeople. We often say that you have to feel them, smell them, taste them, watch them, listen to them—essentially, everything that they do needs to be observed on a regular basis. They need to know that somebody is there to help them.

Let's take a look at the key functions of a sales manager that, when done well, will build a team of sales superstars.

- *Establishing expectations.* What are the requirements of each sales position? What are the goals? What are the expectations of the company in terms of revenue, margin, performance, and key performance indicators? How will each salesperson be evaluated? What measurement tools will be used? What are the requirements for success (what you

Definitions

- *Management*: Establishing policies and procedures

- *Supervision*: Ensuring adherence to policy, procedures, and budgets

- *Leadership*: Inspiring others toward peak performance

have to do to rank in the top performers), and even job retention (what you have to do to avoid getting fired)?

If you have benchmarked the position (as recommended in Strategy Three), you will have already defined those expectations. The next step is to understand and be able to communicate the strategies and tactics necessary to perform at the expected level or higher.

- *Providing feedback against those expectations.* Understand and observe the behaviors and performance of each of your salespeople and offer ongoing, timely, relevant feedback. Many sales managers will offer feedback once a month, sometimes only once or twice a year, but by then it's too late. If the salesperson is doing something wrong, the behavior is already ingrained and will be difficult to change—and the damage to the company has been done. To be effective, feedback must be given immediately or as close to immediately as possible.

Managers get the behaviors they either reward or tolerate. The behaviors you reward with financial compensation, praise, and other recognition will likely be repeated. When you fail

> *"A person who can't lead and won't follow makes a dandy roadblock."*
>
> —Unknown

to give feedback, you are in effect saying that you are willing to tolerate whatever the salespeople are doing—whether it's good or bad. And if that behavior is not what you really want, you have no one to blame but yourself.

Why Sales Managers Fail

When sales managers fail, you'll usually find one or more of the following as the reason (and if you're a salesperson, you've probably worked for and quit managers with one or more of these characteristics):

- *They are unprepared.* They have never been trained in the special skill of managing salespeople, and yet they have been mistakenly thrust into the role of sales manager without the proper foundation.

- *They have poor interpersonal skills.* They are introverts and don't truly enjoy working with or even just being around people.

- *They are selfish.* They take all the credit for the success of their team, don't acknowledge their team's contributions, and essentially ignore the salespeople who are actually doing the work.

- *They are unable to rebound from setbacks.* They take rejection or failure personally and are negative in their thinking and approach. When they are knocked down, they don't know how to get back up.

- *They have a fear of taking decisive action.* Sometimes they are indifferent; other times they are anxious or even frightened about having to make a decision.

- *They lack systematic thinking.* They don't have a process for approaching situations that need to be managed.

- *They have insufficient tools.* They do not possess the behaviors, attributes, or value structure necessary for success in a sales management role.

Why Sales Managers Succeed

Successful sales managers share most, if not all, of these habits:

- *They recruit constantly and consistently.* They are always on the lookout for top candidates, whether or not they have an immediate opening.

- *They hire with caution and care.* They have a proven process for hiring, they hire the whole person, and they make their selections based on assessments, benchmarking, and tools such as the TriMetrix.

- *They create an environment unique for each salesperson.* They treat everyone fairly but differently, based on individual talents, abilities, and motivators.

- *They study their salespeople.* They constantly observe how their people perform, what they do well, what they do poorly.

- *They spend time in the field.* They are engaged with their team. They travel, observe, assist, and coach.

- *They employ systems and tools.* They have proven processes for doing all the things that need to be done to achieve the desired results.

- *Hiring.* The sales manager should play a pivotal role in hiring salespeople. The human resources team can help with the initial screening, administering the assessment, and conducting the background check, but the sales manager should have the final word in who to hire—and who not to hire. Of course, it is absolutely critical that the sales manager understand the job benchmark and what a top performing salesperson in the culture will look like. You don't want sales managers who just hire people they like or who are like themselves; they have to go deeper than that and hire the best people for the job.

- *Teaching and coaching.* Teaching and coaching are the mentoring side of the sales management process that many salespeople simply don't like to do—but they will blossom when their sales manager does it. We'll discuss this further in Strategy Twelve.

Methods of Leadership

There's leadership—and then there's leadership. You can do it poorly, you can do it adequately, or you can do it well. Let's take a look at the various methods of leadership, from most to least effective.

- *Example.* The most effective way to lead is by example, and *you* should set the example. People remember and follow much more of what they see and experience than what they hear, read, or are told. And most people automatically reject a leader whose message is "Do as I say, not as I do." You have to demonstrate your belief in whatever your organization requires by walking the talk, as the cliché says.
- *Encouragement.* The second most powerful way to lead is by encouraging others. Let your people see that you believe in their ability and you want them to succeed. Provide positive reinforcement when they do something well, gentle correction when it's necessary, and assistance when appropriate.
- *Motivation.* One person cannot motivate another—you can't make your salespeople be motivated. You can't want more for them than they want for themselves. But if you have taken the time to understand them, to know them inside and out, you

> "The pessimist complains about the wind. The optimist expects it to change. The leader adjusts the sails."
> — John Maxwell

can guide them to motivate themselves to achieve their own personal best.

· *Expertise.* Subject matter experts are often recognized as leaders—but they can also be annoying and even offensive. If you choose to lead based on your expertise, avoid adopting a superior or condescending attitude.

· *Position/Authority.* Remember when your mother would resort to, "Because I'm the mom and I said so" when she didn't want to discuss something? Leaders who depend on position or authority for their leadership style are taking the same approach: "Because I'm the boss, and I said so." It doesn't inspire people to follow you.

· *Determination.* This is leading by sheer brute strength, and it's the least effective leadership method. It's not bringing people up; it's beating them down.

Develop a leadership style that uses example, encouragement, and motivation. Do an analysis of yourself, and if you're using expertise, position/authority, or determination, make some changes.

Compensating Your Sales Team

Pay plans are essential to sales performance and should, ultimately, determine how much of what gets sold. Salespeople will sell what they make the most money on and/or what is the easiest to sell because they can expect to sell more of those items and that will affect their compensation and performance ranking. They will go where they can make the most money with the least resistance.

Let your sales team tell you what they can do. Don't let them snow you or sandbag you or mess with you in any way—get them to tell you what they can do if they have the right tools and leadership. Then you can push them a little bit to stretch beyond that and provide a reward if they do. The logic behind this is that people will support what they have a part in creating, so if your salespeople have a hand in developing their compensation plan, they're going to be much more likely to respond to it.

What incentive do your salespeople have to expend enough effort to be very competitive? What is your bonus plan tied to?

Sales Pay Plans That Don't Work

We know from our own personal experience as well as thorough study that the following sales pay plans are not effective:

- *Base salaries with no incentives.* Salaried salespeople with no incentive will be order-takers; they have no motivation to go the extra mile.
- *Commission-only.* We believe salespeople should never be paid on straight commission, especially initially, because it drives their focus to survival, not the customer. When this happens, even salespeople with strong potential can get trapped in the lower 25 percent of your team. Once they are established, many top performing salespeople would prefer to be on straight commission because they can make more money. You may want to consider that, but we don't recommend it.
- *Base salary with bonus determined by corporate profitability.* This can work if your sales force really works as a team and the individuals actually have some influence on profitability. But corporate profitability is influenced by so many factors outside the salesperson's control that it is extremely difficult to find salespeople who will be motivated by such a plan.

> "The truth is that many people set rules to keep from making decisions. Not me. I don't want to be a manager or a dictator. I want to be a leader—and leadership is ongoing, adjustable, flexible, and dynamic."
>
> —Mike Krzyzewski

Fair But Different

A good sales manager will treat people fairly but differently. Every salesperson needs to be treated in terms of what his strengths are and what motivates him—and that won't be the same for every member of your team. Get to know all your people, study their assessment profiles, talk with them, spend time with them, and treat them all in whatever way is likely to produce the best results.

Compensation Plan Tips

Here's what to keep in mind as you develop your sales compensation plan: Pay plans must feed an accountability culture. The compensation plan can't stand alone; it must drive people toward accountability. So the plan needs to be specific, clear, and spelled out in writing. And you must be sure each salesperson understands the plan.

Allow new salespeople time to learn, assimilate, and apply new knowledge. This is why straight commission plans are so hard on salespeople, especially in the beginning. They need time to assimilate knowledge and information, to learn and understand your culture. Don't starve them while they are coming up to speed. And even once they are up to speed, they need to invest time in continuing education and various personal and professional development activities, as well as some administrative, support, and even customer service functions. The base salary should compensate them for the time those activities take.

A base salary should reward salespeople for being productive team members. It should make them feel that they are not giving up an income-producing opportunity to help someone else on the team.

This is one of the most important points we make in this book: *Hire the best salespeople you can afford,* pay them a base salary that is sufficient for them to live on, and a commission that is attractive, provides incentive, and will require them to stretch. Negotiate that with each individual salesperson, keeping in mind that some people are more money-motivated than others. Yes, that means each salesperson could conceivably have a different pay plan, which is an accounting nightmare. But do you want to let your accounting department run your sales team? Of course not.

Your compensation plans should be built around the individual's performance. You can have everyone on the same base salary if you want, but the actual bonuses need to be performance-based and they need to be designed based on the individual's production and potential. That means some of your salespeople will make more money than others, but that's because some are better than others. Everyone on your sales team will not be exactly the same, which means they shouldn't be working under a pay plan that is exactly the same. Go back to each individual's assessment, figure out what their personal drivers are, and come up with a plan that works for each one.

Let's say you have a team of three salespeople, and you pay them each a base salary of $25,000 plus a bonus that is essentially a commission on sales that exceed a certain level or pass a designated goal. You can decide how that bonus is calculated—is it based on gross sales, net sales, profitability or what? It's up to you. Once you've figured that out, you take a look at each individual team member.

One salesperson has a very dense territory that requires very little travel between calls and the demographics indicate there are a lot of prospective customers in the area. The second has a very spread out territory and will have to spend a larger percentage of time traveling between calls. The third's territory is dense like the first, but it doesn't have as many prospective customers in it. Each one of those reps should have goals and compensation customized for their particular circumstances. The first one shouldn't make more simply because he's got the best territory, the second one shouldn't be penalized for the fact that he has no choice but to spend a lot of time traveling, and the third one shouldn't make less because his territory doesn't have as much potential. In this example, the first rep should have higher goals than the second and third reps. The rate of the commission can be the same, but at what level of performance the payments kick in should be different.

You might also set tiers for the bonuses. For example, for the first X number of dollars (or units or whatever measurement you use) above the individual goal, the commission is 5 percent. For the next X number of dollars, it's 10 percent. And maybe for everything above the goal plus the first two amounts, it's 15 percent. Those percentages and the points at which they kick in should be negotiated individually.

What do you do with a rep who says, "Wait a minute. So-and-so is getting 12 percent, I'm only getting 10, I want 12."? Simple. You negotiate what that salesperson has to do to earn 12 percent and adjust your agreement accordingly.

Finally, don't punish your successful people by restricting how much they can make. We have seen companies reduce sales commissions for high performers because someone decided the salespeople were making too much money. The president of one company told a top salesperson, "You are making more money at a commission rate of 5 percent than my key executives, so we're cutting the rate to 2.5 percent." The salesperson pointed out—quite logically—that if he was making money, so was the company. But the executives didn't see it that way; they were just looking at the bottom line of his compensation. So they cut the commission and the salesperson quit. Both sides lost, but the salesperson bounced back quicker.

There will be times when you have valid reasons for restructuring the compensation plan. You may have new products, operational issues, or other circumstances to consider. You may want to change the compensation to alter the behavior of the salespeople—for example, if you want them to focus on a particular product, you might increase the commission rate on that item. You may need to decrease the rate on certain items if they have become unprofitable. But when you have a sales compensation plan that is profitable for the company and provides sufficient incentive to your team, don't try to change it just to reduce the amount of money your people can make.

Salespeople can handle change, but they don't like what they call cheap shot changes, which is change just for the sake of changing or changes that will reduce their ability to make money based on their performance. Treat your salespeople with fairness and respect, and they will respond with high performance.

——— KEY LESSONS ———

* The best sales managers tend to come from the ranks of average salespeople.

* The role of the sales manager is to set the standards for performance and hold the sales team accountable.

* If you have top sales performers who are expecting to move into management, do them and your company a favor by redirecting their career expectations.

* Salespeople don't quit jobs or companies; they quit managers.

* There are two types of sales managers: selling and nonselling. Nonselling sales managers tend to deliver more value and benefit to the sales team because they can focus on managing and supporting the salespeople without worrying about their own sales quotas.

* The two primary reasons most companies move their top sales performers into management is because top performers look for a well-defined career path and have come to believe

incorrectly that their career path should include sales management, and because it's easier than looking for a qualified sales manager.

* Often a midlevel sales performer can be groomed for successful management. If you decide to do this, make sure your top performers understand that this is in no way a negative reflection on them or their abilities. You may choose to hire salespeople that you don't think will rise to the top because they have the qualities you want in a sales manager.

* Sales managers should be trained; don't expect them to automatically know how to do the job. The most effective way to train sales managers is to retain a sales and sales management training firm.

* The key sales management functions include establishing expectations, providing feedback against those expectations, hiring, teaching, and coaching.

* When sales managers fail, it is because they are unprepared, have poor personal skills, are selfish, are unable to rebound from setbacks, have a fear of taking decisive action, lack systematic thinking, and have insufficient tools.

* When sales managers succeed, it is because they recruit constantly and consistently, hire with caution and care, create an environment unique for each salesperson, study their salespeople, spend time in the field, and employ systems and tools.

* The various methods of leadership, from most effective to least effective, are example, encouragement, motivation, expertise, position/authority, and determination.

* Sales pay plans that don't work are base salaries with no incentives, commission-only, and base salary with bonus determined by corporate profitability.

＊ Effective compensation plan tips include designing a plan that feeds an accountability culture, paying new salespeople while they are learning and assimilating, having a base salary that rewards salespeople for being productive team members, building pay plans around individual performance, and not punishing your successful people by restricting how much they can make.

Coach, Coach, Coach

Effective sales managers are great coaches. They might not be spectacular salespeople, but they know how to help the salespeople on their teams reach superstar status. Good sales managers also teach and train, but their real strength, the reason they get results, comes from their coaching ability.

It's important to understand the significant differences between teaching, training, and coaching. Each is important and they may sometimes overlap, but they are different functions. Let's take a look at each one:

Teaching is typically done in a classroom setting or some other type of organized setting where you are covering specific concepts and theories. In the process, you may also share insight from your own experiences and demonstrate practical applications of the concepts and theories. Teaching is explaining and showing how things work.

Training is actually imparting the ideas, concepts, or strategies in a safe environment where the student gets a chance to practice or use what has been taught without having to worry about the consequences of a mistake.

Coaching is active involvement in the field. It's spending time with an individual, reinforcing what they know and do well, helping them make corrections when necessary.

Teaching is the why. Training is the how. And coaching is doing in the real world.

The top sales managers do all these things very well, but they are especially proficient in coaching. After all, you can—and should—bring in a teacher or trainer to instruct your team on various sales techniques or product knowledge. That's part of what The Brooks Group does for our clients. But you can't bring a coach in for a one-time class and have it be effective. That's why top sales managers avail themselves of every opportunity to coach their people, to offer insights into how to more effectively use something the salesperson has been taught or trained how to do. They coach in the hallways, between meetings, on the way to a sales call, after a sales call, at lunch—whenever the chance arises.

Again, let's compare this to sports. Players on a football team are taught the fundamentals of blocking and tackling. They are trained on how to perform those fundamentals. Then they are coached to refine and further develop their skills when they perform those fundamentals.

If you sat someone down in a classroom and said, "This is how you tackle another player," your student would probably understand. You can go through the steps: Hit the ball carrier as low as you can, not high on the body; keep your head on the downfield side of the ball carrier's body so you have the strength of your entire body to pull him down; stay on your feet; keep your feet planted and moving; once you make contact with the ball carrier, wrap your arms around him, then drive him back and up to get him off his feet.

Even if you have absolutely no interest in football, you now know how to tackle. You may have never done it, you may not ever do it, but you know how. If you want to play football, the next step is training—getting out on the field where you can put on the shoulder pads, helmet, cleated shoes, maybe gloves and other equipment, and practice these fundamentals in a safe environment with your own team when a game is not at stake. And then the coaching begins. The coach evaluates what you did, tells you what was good and what wasn't (or asks you to figure that out to see if you understand), and works with you on how you can improve and further develop the fundamentals.

> *"Help others solve their problems; standing farther away, you can often see matters more clearly than they do. The greatest service you can render someone is helping him help himself."*
> —Baltasar Gracian

This is what the best sales managers do with all their people. They make sure they have an understanding of how their people perform and that their people understand why they are performing as they are, and then the sales manager helps them perform to the best of their abilities. When you have a whole person assessment on an individual as we discussed in Strategy Two, you can be a more effective coach because you'll be able to help them understand their current and ideal situation, then help them move closer to their full potential.

Principles of Effective Coaching

Even people who are naturally good coaches can benefit from studying specific coaching techniques and strategies, and they are comfortable applying these principles to the relationships they have with the people they are coaching. These are the principles of effective coaching:

- *Be willing to make others look good.* Leaders and sales managers are there to serve their people, to help their salespeople perform at their optimal level. You have to be willing to remove yourself from the spotlight and put your top performers in that place instead.

- *Do more than talk.* People learn from what they experience and do, not from what they hear. If you as a sales manager are going to be a great coach, you have to get out, work with your team, be with them, ride with them, travel with them, and meet their customers and their prospects. You've got to get out from behind your desk. You can't teach what you don't know, and you can't lead where you won't go. So get out and spend time with your people, see what they are experiencing, see how they handle different sales situations, and be prepared to offer guidance.

- *Be up, even when others are down.* This can be difficult and sometimes requires some strong acting skills. Your salespeople are looking to you to be their support mechanism, to help them, and to boost them. Sometimes you have to appear happy and upbeat when you really don't feel like it. But it goes with the territory—it's just something you have to do.

- *Use systems and principles, not rigid how-to's.* People will respond to you better if you explain the reasons behind what you're recommending. They like to understand the why followed by the how. Don't just tell them what to do—tell them why you're making the suggestion and then how to do it.

- *Be inspiring.* Be someone your salespeople trust, feel comfortable with, and want to share their experiences

> "The mediocre teacher tells. The good teacher explains. The superior teacher demonstrates. The great teacher inspires."
> —William A. Ward

with. Let them know by your actions, not just words, that you have their best interests at heart.

We can't emphasize this enough: Coaching is more than just being physically present; it's active involvement. And that involvement has to be constant. You've got to be around your salespeople all the time. You've got to understand each of them as individuals. You've got to know what drives them, what excites them, what they're good at, what they need help developing. And with every possible engagement, you've got to be able to offer guidance to help them improve so they can be as good as they possibly can.

Attention from the sales manager shouldn't be an unusual thing or a big deal. It should be regular, routine, and something the salespeople look forward to. We talked with a sales rep who told us that she had a sales manager early in her career who only

When a Sales Manager Isn't Necessary

If you have a sales manager who simply gathers data and makes reports about where the reps are in terms of their goals, you don't need that person on your staff—at least, not in the role of sales manager. Because that's not managing sales, it's accounting. Any executive can call the various salespeople and ask what their numbers are or—even easier—just review the company's sales report.

Senior management and executives don't need a sales manager to tell them what they can read for themselves—but salespeople need a sales manager who coach and mentor them, and companies need a sales manager who can help develop the sales team. Make sure the sales managers in your organization are doing what they should be doing.

communicated with her when she made a mistake. His attitude was that if all was going well, she didn't need to hear from him. He was absolutely wrong—and she did not realize until she had moved on to a different company what a powerful resource an effective sales manager can be for a salesperson's personal and professional development.

Effective coaching demands a system or process inside of which meaningful coaching can occur. A sales philosophy is essential, along with a linked and sequential sales process reflecting that philosophy. The sales philosophy provides the foundation for sales performance, and everyone on the sales team should know what it is. What is your sales philosophy? Remember, the "why to" always drives "how to."

Creating a Culture of Motivated Salespeople

You cannot motivate your salespeople; they must motivate themselves. But you can create an environment in which this motivation can occur. You can create a culture where the self-motivated excel.

> *"Coaches have to watch for what they don't want to see and listen to what they don't want to hear."*
> —John Madden

Though you cannot make someone else be motivated, you must also recognize that everybody is motivated by something, and the sales manager needs to uncover what that motivation is for the people on the team—and hope that the motivation is something that is rewarded within the company's culture.

There are two key motivators for most salespeople: One is, of course, money. The other is the excitement and thrill of success, the buzz they get from winning. Many salespeople are also motivated by being seen as a value resource and partner to their prospects and customers.

Achievement Culture

An achievement culture is one where salespeople compete against their own previous best. They establish their own goals. They have skin in the game, so to speak. They own the goal. It's theirs, and if they don't reach it, it's no one's fault but their own. An achievement culture promotes healthy competition—competition where the salespeople are not concerned about beating each other but about beating their own previous performance and doing that better than anyone else. And the reward system provides incentives for the salespeople who are constantly improving and performing better.

Competitive Culture

A competitive culture is one where people individually or collectively compete against each other. Build it very carefully because it can backfire on you. In a competitive culture, people tend to be less concerned with improving their own skills and performance and more concerned with just outdoing someone else.

Avoid too many contests, particularly those with only one winner where the prize is based solely on total sales. In those circumstances, we typically see that the winner isn't necessarily the best salesperson but the craftiest—and not always the one with the most integrity. The others know that, and they resent it. For example, an experienced salesperson could see the contest announcement and sandbag it by calling his customers and saying, "We've got a contest going. Please hold your orders and place them on this date." He'll win the contest without doing anything to actually improve his own performance. The other salespeople will likely know what he did and know that they had no chance of winning, so when the next contest is announced, they don't bother trying. The end result is that the contest did more harm than good. Rather than boosting moral and performance, you've done some serious damage to the team. Another downside to these types of contests is that they drive the focus away from the customer and toward the spiff. You might get a short-term burst of activity, but it won't be sustainable.

Many companies hold sales contests much like they have sales on their merchandise. Typically, things are put on sale because they're not moving at the regular price for whatever reason. Companies will consider a sales contest because the salespeople aren't performing at the desired level and management thinks a contest will be motivating. But that only incentivizes salespeople to try to make people buy what they don't really want—and in the long run, that will blow up on you. What's more, you cannot motivate people who are demotivated, and if you try to do that with a contest, you'll likely only demotivate them further.

Another reason a strongly competitive culture is risky is that it's human nature for people to not want to help their competitors. If your salespeople are all striving to win the same prize, they're not going to be inclined to share what they know and what they've learned with the others. If they're going after individual prizes for individual performance, they're more likely to help each other.

Even though we just recommended avoiding too many sales contests, we want to point out that sales contests can be great tools if they are structured properly. They help keep the competitive juices flowing—especially when the primary competition is oneself. We recommend different reward levels and categories so that the salespeople can continue to develop as well-rounded professionals, not single-minded warriors. At the same time, don't set the bar so low that everyone wins. You don't get a prize just for

> *"A good coach will make his players see what they can be rather than what they are."*
>
> —Ara Parasheghian

showing up—that's an attendance reward; it's not recognizing a winner.

If you want to have contests, set them up so that each salesperson is competing against his own personal best and striving to improve in the areas where he is most challenged. Make the prize individual as well—cash for the person who is motivated by cash, a trip for the person who is motivated by recreation, time off for the

Bean Counters and Bonuses

Whatever incentives you offer your salespeople—whether cash, trips, merchandise, or time off—are going to cost you money. And when something costs you money, you can expect your accounting people to fight you on it. You have to educate them on the value of rewarding your sales team.

The last time we revised the sales bonus plan at JK Harris & Company, our senior financial advisor and our executive vice president of sales did battle over it. The finance guy couldn't believe how much we wanted to pay out in bonuses. He focused on how much the sales consultants could earn rather than on the real bottom line, which was that the company's revenue and profits would increase as well, and those bonuses would be money well-spent.

A client of The Brooks Group had to fight his financial officer when he decided to give each of his top sales performers a new BMW 325i. Now, the requirements to get the car were strenuous, but 15 of the 18 salespeople made it. Was it expensive? Sure, but the cost was worth it because the company more than covered the expense in increased revenue and profits.

When you set up your incentive programs, do the math to be sure the company will still be making money after you pay the bonuses. Then show the value to your bean counters to get them to buy into the idea.

person who finds that an incentive and so on. Use the whole person assessment to help you structure the details for each participant—the goals, measurements, and rewards. Yes, this approach is more work, but the results are worth it.

Accountability Culture

An accountability culture is one where all salespeople feel answerable for their own actions and results. You build it through regular reporting systems:

- *Activity (weekly).* This is a report of the specific things the salesperson has actually done—phone calls, face-to-face calls, networking events, prospecting efforts, and so on.
- *Sales (monthly).* This is the report of the actual sales—the number of units or whatever measure you use. It's the sales production report.
- *Job coaching/review (twice annually).* This is the formal performance review. If the sales manager is doing regular ongoing coaching, the content of this review will never be a surprise; it will simply be a summary of the reporting period.

One of the drawbacks to an accountability culture is that it's easy to focus more on the reports than on actual performance. A salesperson told us that he had worked for a company that would chastise sales reps if they did not meet their activity quotas, even if they were meeting or exceeding sales quotas. "We were required to make 45 sales calls a week, and if we didn't, we heard about it," he said. "If we had a week with several calls that took an unusually long time and we were going to come up short, we would log in 'calls' on the clerk at the gas station or the server in a restaurant. It was crazy, and it forced us to be dishonest." When he changed companies, he asked his new manager about the call quota. The sales manager said, "You don't have a call quota. I'm not paying you to make calls, I'm paying you to make sales." He was still required to turn in weekly activity reports, but he was measured and compensated on his production.

As a side note, it's true that activity has a direct correlation to the overall sales performance. If a salesperson's sales start to slide, take a look at his activity report to see how he's spending his time and use that information for coaching if appropriate. But don't get obsessed with activity—your focus should be on sales.

Which culture is best? We believe the achievement culture is most effective. What we actually see most often in the real world is a combination of the competitive and accountability cultures. Companies often try to call that an achievement culture because some managers believe that meeting your numbers counts as achievement, and the reward for that is you get to keep your job. But sales managers who are great coaches know better.

KEY LESSONS

* Effective sales managers are good teachers and trainers, and great coaches.

* Teaching is explaining and showing how things work; training is imparting ideas, concepts, or strategies in a safe environment where the student gets a chance to practice without worrying about making a mistake; coaching is active involvement in the field.

* Effective coaches are willing to make others look good; do more than talk; are up even when others are down; use systems and principles, not rigid how-to's; and are inspiring.

* Sales managers cannot motivate their salespeople; the salespeople must motivate themselves. However, sales managers can create an environment where the self-motivated excel.

* Avoid holding too many sales contests, especially those with only one winner where the prize is based solely on total sales.

* Expect your bean counters to resist paying salespeople substantial bonuses, commissions, and other rewards. Be prepared to demonstrate how those incentives pay off in increased sales and profitability.

* An achievement culture is one where salespeople compete again their own previous best. A competitive culture is one where people individually or collectively compete against each other. An accountability culture is one where all salespeople feel answerable for their own actions and results. An achievement culture is the most effective.

Establish Expectations and Measure Outcomes

E very one of your salespeople needs to know exactly what is expected of them and how they will be measured and evaluated—and they need to be told from day one so there is never any question. The way to do this is with a strong orientation that is provided for each salesperson so all salespeople start out on the right foot when they join the company. You want to get them up to speed as quickly as possible, and one of the ways to do that is to very clearly define their role.

Strategy Three—benchmarking—will help you do this. If you've done a good benchmark, you know what their role looks like, and that knowledge will help you create a meaningful orientation process. You don't want to leave them alone and allow them to stumble, get discouraged, or develop bad habits.

Get Off on the Right Foot

Lay the groundwork for success for each salesperson from the moment the job offer is extended and accepted by beginning the orientation process immediately. While we're focusing on how to do this with salespeople, this strategy can and should be applied to all new hires in your company. Stay in touch during the period between the time the job has been accepted and the new hire reports to work. While this isn't a formal orientation, it is still an opportunity to begin introducing your company to the new employee.

Send an agenda prior to the first day so the new salesperson knows what to expect. Be sure he knows who to see when he arrives and has a schedule. Make sure your receptionist and key co-workers know the new person is starting and will welcome him appropriately. It's also a good idea to assign a mentor or partner, someone who can take the new person on a facility tour, show him his work space, take him to lunch on the first day, and be a resource for him in those early days as he's getting on a firm footing with the organization. Then, of course, provide ongoing mentoring as appropriate.

Remember that first impressions count. Just as a poor first impression can doom a sales call, a poor first impression made by your company on a new hire can have a negative impact on that person's career with you. Have a meaningful, in-depth orientation program, keeping in mind that orientation is an ongoing process, not a one-day, one-time event. Done poorly, it can lead to frustration and the equivalent of buyer's remorse—the salesperson regretting the decision to come on board. Don't assume that if a salesperson is knowledgeable and experienced, he'll figure things out—take the time to tell him what he needs to know. Orientation establishes how an employee frames his or her ongoing employment standards. Start with the basics—people become productive sooner if they are firmly grounded in the basic knowledge they need to understand their job.

A key part of orientation is to familiarize new hires with your culture. Culture is what is done every single day in the company, and it's usually set from the top. Many companies have a formal structure that is organized and published—then they have an informal structure of how things actually get done that might have little to do with the formal structure. All of this is part of the culture and needs to be communicated to new hires.

Introduce new hires to all the appropriate people so that they know who to see for their various needs and to handle issues that may arise. And provide them with a written list of the names, titles, and contact information of these people so they have something to refer to later.

> *"Treat people as if they were what they ought to be and you help them become what they are capable of being."*
> —Johann Wolfgang von Goethe

It's also important to immediately teach new hires all required rules and regulations, especially the ones that need to be followed on a daily basis. Don't let ignorance cause a new hire to make a mistake that could harm the company or his career.

Top Five Orientation Needs for Salespeople

While every new employee needs to learn about the company and its basic rules, their job, expectations, and how they will be measured, some positions require different orientation details. Here are the top five orientation needs of salespeople:

1. *Product training.* Obviously, salespeople need to know what the product is, how to sell it in their market, and scenarios in which the product is most appropriate. They need a clear understanding of how your product compares to competitors'. There is no excuse for salespeople to lack product knowledge—absolutely none.

2. *Operations orientation.* Salespeople need to understand the various functions of operations and how those operations

are performed. What parts of operations do they need to be aware of and how do those parts relate to their job?

3. *Orientation process.* Show them the various tools available to them and ensure they are used. Introduce them to the right people, and make sure they are comfortable with the resources you've provided.

4. *Technology.* Show the new salesperson how the company uses technology, including the computer log-in, e-mail, messaging, intranet, electronic reports, expense reports, contact management software, and so on. Make sure they know how to use all the programs they will be required to use in carrying out their sales function. Don't assume they know anything. This is especially important if you have proprietary systems that aren't available on the open market.

5. *Sales skills.* Even experienced salespeople need to be taught how things are done at your company, including successful sourcing strategies, client segmentation, sales strategies, marketing tools and resources.

Orientation Don'ts

There are some specific things you must not do in the orientation process. Do not:

· *Leave new salespeople to "sink or swim" on their own.* Certainly you want to hire people who show initiative, but don't throw them into the deep end of your pool without teaching them to swim first—even if they know how to swim in someone else's pool. New salespeople should be welcomed and absorbed into the team as quickly as possible. Leaving them alone to flounder on their own can be very expensive and high risk.

· *Overwhelm them with too much, too soon.* Much like in the actual sales process where you ask feedback questions to make sure the prospect is staying with you, get feedback from your new hires to make sure they are absorbing and processing the material you are providing. Make sure they are mastering each point before you move on to the next.

> *"It's hard to win if you don't know what winning looks like. Make sure everyone knows what it's going to take to win."*
> —JK Harris

- *Allow them to wing it.* Don't let new salespeople come in with preconceived notions about what will work in your environment. Make sure they are not bringing bad habits that won't work in your culture or that might jeopardize their successful performance with your organization.

- *Assign busy work that has nothing to do with their core assignment because you're having a busy week.* Don't give a new salesperson busy work just because you're busy and feel like you don't have time to conduct a proper orientation—it's degrading and demoralizing. Whatever you give them to do

Benefits of a Good Orientation Experience

- *Reduced startup costs.* Employees are up to speed and productive quickly.

- *Reduced anxiety.* Employees feel comfortable entering into an unknown situation.

- *Reduced turnover.* Employees feel valued and have the tools and support needed to succeed, so they are less likely to see opportunities elsewhere.

- *Sets the right tone.* Employees develop realistic job expectations and the right mind-set.

should be targeted and specific to the role they will have with your company.

· *Think it's someone else's job.* As the sales manager, don't ever think that providing orientation to your new salespeople is someone else's job. It's not HR's job, nor is it the CEO's, the VP of sales', or another salesperson's—it's the sales manager's job. Certainly there are places for these other people to participate in the orientation, but the sales manager is in charge and responsible for the process.

Hold Salespeople Accountable

To hold salespeople accountable, you must create and use objective measurement systems, and the salespeople need to understand those systems. Salespeople need to know how they will be measured, what they are expected to achieve, and what strategies and tactics they should use to reach their goals. The right activities will breed the right results. When you're not getting the desired results and you know you've hired the right people, make the appropriate and necessary adjustments. Figure out what isn't working—is it the process, the trainer, the mentor, or what? Figure that out, and change what needs to be changed.

When you fail to hold salespeople accountable, you are reinforcing the notion that any behavior and result is acceptable. And unless you tell people otherwise, how can they know that what they're doing isn't acceptable?

Begin with establishing easy-to-monitor performance standards that ensure a person is

> "Everyone has got it in him, if he will only make up his mind and stick at it. None of us is born with a stop-valve on his powers or with a set limit to his capacities. There is no limit possible to the expansion of each one of us."
>
> —Charles Schwab

moving toward the successful achievement of the predetermined sales objectives. Those standards might include the completion of identified measurable activities, such as the number of calls or presentations, completion of training programs, demonstrated competencies relative to specific activities, and sales volume. Note that we mention sales volume last—that's because the successful completion of other things will naturally lead to sales volume. Measure actual performance against established standards using a reporting system that works in your environment. When performance falls short of expectations, address the issue immediately.

> *"The best leaders are those most interested in surrounding themselves with assistants and associates smarter than they are. They are frank in admitting this and are willing to pay for such talents."*
> —Amos Parrish

You've probably heard the saying, "Don't let the inmates run the asylum." It's a good philosophy to adopt when it comes to your sales team because a lack of accountability guarantees they will. Holding them accountable keeps you in charge and in control.

Hold the Sales Managers Accountable, Too

Just as you hold your salespeople accountable for their performance, you also need to hold your sales managers accountable as well. In addition to measuring them by the performance of the salespeople they manage, you should also set expectations for their own behavior. Are they spending a sufficient amount of time in the field, working shoulder-to-shoulder with their people? Are they teaching, training, and coaching? Do they operate with honesty and integrity? Are they positive and upbeat? A negative manager will corrupt your sales force. Do they respect boundaries and confidential information? A manager who gossips will wreck your sales force.

Activity That Can Be Monitored and Measured

- Self-generated prospects
- Earned referrals
- Contact referrals
- Face-to-face appointments scheduled
- Telephone presentations made
- Face-to-face presentations made

- Completed sales
- Volume
- Margin
- Vertical integration
- Sales cycle time

Just as you can't afford a salesperson who isn't meeting expectations, you can't afford a sales manager who isn't doing the job.

Dealing with Sales Demotivators

As you focus on keeping your salespeople performing at their best, it's important to understand what will work against your efforts. If you see any these sales demotivators among your team, address them immediately and individually. And if you see one, you'll likely see others because most of them are interrelated.

- *Too much routine.* This could be just doing the same thing over and over, or it could be excessive, unproductive, repetitive busy work, rather than actual selling. Many times things that are done routinely are not necessary, but they've become tradition. Look at the things your salespeople do regularly, and be sure they have value. Remember that having to do the same thing over and over can become tedious and boring for high-energy salespeople, and it will kill their drive.

· *Fatigue and overwork.* When people are tired on a long-term basis, they can't perform at their best. If your people aren't getting sufficient rest and time off, look at what they're doing. Are they working smart—or just hard? Do they understand their role? Are they properly trained? The American business culture has historically been one where workaholics get ahead, but if your sales team is finding work more fatiguing than energizing, you need to make some changes. People need breaks—they need time away from the job to rest and restore themselves.

· *Negative thinking.* It is the nature of successful salespeople to be positive, so when you have someone who is seeing only the bad side of things, you need to find out why.

· *Fear.* Fear is a potentially paralyzing emotion; it can easily stop a salesperson from taking action.

· *Scapegoating.* Assigning blame rather than accepting responsibility can make people tentative and overly cautious. If you or others in your group tend to cast blame on others, you'll see a drop in the entire team's motivation level.

· *Unfair pay plan.* First, be sure that your pay plan is based on individual performance (see Strategy Eleven). Second, make sure everyone understands how the plan is structured. Third, check the plan for fairness and be sure no one can coast under it. It's easy to say that if people feel they are being fairly compensated, they shouldn't care what other people are getting, but that's just not how people are. If you have people who are doing less work but getting paid more, it will have an impact on everyone—and the people who are being paid less will likely start working less.

· *Team incompatibility.* When people feel like they don't fit, they find it hard to perform at their best. And even adults can behave childishly when personality conflicts are involved.

- *Poor economy.* A down economy can lead to reduced sales and revenue, and a general feeling that no one will buy because nobody has any money—and that will feed negative thinking.
- *Low consumer confidence.* This ties into the emotional impact of the economy. When overall consumer confidence is down, whether or not it is actually affecting your sales, it can affect the morale of your sales team.
- *Lack of clear direction.* This could be either a lack of clear direction from management or personal direction on the part of a salesperson, or a combination of both. It's not knowing where you are going and not having a plan to get there.
- *Too much change.* People can accept and even embrace necessary change, but change for the sake of changing can be unnerving.
- *Changing focus or direction.* Again, people can accept a new focus or direction, but it must be based on sound logic and reason, not a haphazard knee-jerk reaction to something.
- *Poor quality.* When anything your sales team has to deal with is of poor quality—whether it's working conditions, management, situations, product, or service—it can be demotivating.
- *Unrealistic goals.* Goals that are simply not feasible don't make salespeople work harder; they make them give up because there's no point in trying.
- *Favoritism.* Is it natural that a sales manager is going to like some salespeople more than others? Sure. But don't give the ones you like advantages over the others.
- *General mood of the sales team and management.* Moods are

contagious, and if the mood on your team is down, your salespeople will be demotivated.

───── KEY LESSONS ─────

✳ From day one, all your salespeople need to know exactly what is expected of them and how they will be measured and evaluated.

✳ Have a meaningful, in-depth orientation program.

✳ Begin the orientation process for new salespeople as soon as the job offer is extended and accepted. Stay in touch during the period between the time the offer is accepted and the new sales rep reports to work. Send an agenda prior to the first day. Assign a mentor. Introduce new hires to all the appropriate people so they know who they need to see for whatever issues might arise. Teach the new hires all the required rules and regulations.

✳ The top five orientation needs for salespeople are product training, operations orientation, a general orientation process, technology, and sales skills.

✳ In the orientation process, do *not* leave new salespeople to sink or swim; overwhelm them with too much, too soon; allow them to wing it; assign busy work that has nothing to do with their actual job; think providing orientation is someone else's job.

✳ The benefits of a good orientation experience include reduced startup costs, anxiety, and turnover, and it sets the right tone.

✳ Create and use objective measurement systems, and make sure your salespeople understand them.

✳ Hold sales managers accountable for their performance just as you hold salespeople accountable for theirs.

✳ Sales demotivators include too much routine, fatigue and overwork, negative thinking, fear, scapegoating, unfair pay plan, team incompatibility, poor economy, low consumer confidence, lack of clear direction, too much change, changing focus or direction, poor quality, unrealistic goals, favoritism, and general mood of the sales team and management.

Stay on Track for Success

Selling skills can be taught in a classroom environment initially, but for true mastery, they must be coached, reinforced, and constantly upgraded in the field. To help salespeople reach their maximum potential, sales managers must learn how to give feedback that results in continuous improvement; how to provide ongoing training in the form of classes, coaching, and discussions; and how to handle joint sales calls for maximum effectiveness.

We like to say that selling is both a science and an art. It's a science in that the skills can be taught, and pretty much anyone can learn them. When those skills are practiced well, it becomes an art. But making sales an art requires regular coaching. Taking the football analogy we used in Strategy Twelve a bit further, you can learn how to tackle, you can practice and get good at it, but if you're going to stay good and continue to get better, you need coaching. A coach will make sure you're practicing correctly and doing the right things so that doing the right things becomes automatic.

When salespeople have learned a sequentially linked process, understand the concepts, and are well-coached, they know exactly what to do in every selling situation. There's no having to decide. There's no having to stop and figure out what's happening. It's a matter of recognizing what is happening and intuitively making whatever adjustments are needed.

During the 1970s the Pittsburgh Steelers had 10 offensive plays. Other teams at the time had more, and today, professional football teams have many more offensive plays, but back then, the Steelers had 10. Chuck Noll was the coach, and at practice every day, he'd run each of those plays 30 to 40 times, until they were so thoroughly ingrained that when the players heard the call, they responded instinctively. Every team in the NFL knew those 10 plays; the Steelers' offense was many things, but it wasn't surprising. In spite of that, the Steelers won four Super Bowls with those 10 offensive plays. Certainly they had good players, but the foundation for their performance was practicing and coaching on the fundamentals, over and over and over. That's what a good sales manager needs to do with his sales team.

> "The attitude of the coach will be the attitude of the players."
>
> —JK Harris

Feedback for Continuous Improvement

Meaningful feedback is done in real time. It's immediate; it's never postponed. Sales managers must have the courage to provide good and constructive feedback quickly and regularly. You have to see it as essential to a salesperson's development, which is why you make time for it; you don't let anything take precedence over it.

Feedback should be given in a positive manner. It should never be insulting, and you should never show anger or frustration. You might, for example, review what the salesperson did and even ask why he did certain things the way he did. Then when you see a place for improvement, suggest a change, perhaps by saying something like, "Think about doing this. Practice it this way, and next time, try it this way, and see what happens." And even if you're thinking it, *never* say anything such as "I can't believe you did something so stupid!"

> "Criticism should not be querulous and wasting, but guiding, instructive, inspiring."
> —Ralph Waldo Emerson

When you make a commitment to giving feedback, your team will know there is going to be consistent feedback about performance, that they're going to hear something every single time you're with them about their performance. And they'll begin to look forward to it. They may not always like what you have to say, but they will look forward to the session.

If you want to help your salespeople accelerate their move from novice to professional, never stop teaching and coaching.

Make These Initiatives Available to Your Team

- Ongoing classes

- Ongoing coaching

- Discussions around successes or failures

- Problem-solving discussions related to specific sales issues

- Joint calls with the sales manager and perhaps even other salespeople— your most valuable coaching tool

Joint Calls

You can't provide effective feedback if you aren't out in the field watching your people work. The way to spend quality time in the sales arena with your team is by making joint calls with them. The key benefits of joint calls include:

- The chance for you to demonstrate caring and appreciation on an individual basis.
- An opportunity to coach in real time because you can give feedback immediately after the call. It's called curbside coaching because you go out to the curb and talk about what happened.
- You'll get firsthand insights into the salesperson's strengths and weaknesses because you'll see him in action.
- You'll stay in contact with customers, which is important for continuity if you do have turnover on your team. Also, the marketplace changes about every 18 months, and you need to know what's going on out there.
- You'll keep your view of the business in perspective. It's easy to lose perspective when you isolate yourself in an office behind a desk. When you're out there in front of the customers, you're able to see the big picture and help steer the organization in the best direction.

Before you make joint calls, set expectations. Talk with your salespeople about why you're going on the calls and what your objectives are. Don't let them sandbag you by only taking you to see customers that love them and see them as the greatest thing in the world. Tell them you don't want to go to their best accounts. You know they have accounts that adore them; you don't need to see that. Instead, let them take you to see customers or prospects that are a challenge, where they don't have a particularly strong relationship so you can help them perform better with those accounts.

Before each call, determine the objectives. What does the sales-person want to accomplish on the call? You also need to establish roles. What is your role in the call? How will the salesperson intro-duce and position you? Are you going to participate or simply observe? If you have decided to be a quiet observer, resist the urge to jump in if you see the salesperson having trouble. Let them know ahead of time that if they really need help, they can ask—otherwise, you're going to let them handle it.

> *"You can't make someone else be motivated. They have to motivate themselves."*
> —Richard D. Dickerson

There may be rare exceptions to that rule—like the situation a sales manager told us about when a young trainee he was working with did a great job on the call but could not figure out how to gra-ciously end the conversation and leave. After about 15 minutes of the trainee repeating what should have been parting words, the sales manager came to the rescue and got them out of there.

When the call is over, objectively evaluate how the salesperson performed and do your curbside coaching.

Spotting Performance Problems

Pay attention to your salespeople so you can spot minor perform-ance issues before they become insurmountable problems. It is much easier to correct someone who is just an inch off course than someone who is miles off course, so don't let your people stray too far before you're working with them to bring them back. Keep in mind that performance issues on the job may be caused by circumstances off the job. While you want to respect the privacy of your salespeople, if something is going on in their personal lives that is having a negative impact on the professional performance, you need to know so you can deal with it. Some of the behaviors you should look for include:

- Subtle, overt, or even extreme changes in attitudes, voice inflections, and appearance
- Slow or even unresponsive to paperwork and projects
- Frequent slipups with customers
- Downturn in productivity and sales numbers
- No communication; they act is if they are trying to avoid you
- Constant complaints that quota is too high and unattainable
- Salesperson does not buy into the sales or promotion plan
- Missing an above average number of days from work
- Salesperson is emotionally flat

When you see any of these behaviors, it's time for a candid, confidential conversation to find out what's going on. Certainly you want to work with people who have done a good job but are experiencing a temporary performance downturn; at the same time, you need to keep the general health of your business in mind. Prepare before you sit down with the person. Consider issues such as tenure, historical performance, the whole person assessment data, and the individual's current situation, including any life changes or stressers. Keep the conversation cordial but frank. Let the salesperson know that if there is a legitimate business issue going on, you want to take the appropriate action. If it's something personal, you may need to practice a little tough love and point out that the company can't afford to carry someone for long who isn't producing and who may be dragging down the rest of the team. If you have an employee assistance program, remind the person of that resource (you should have covered it in orientation). Then set goals and a timetable for improvement, and hold the person accountable.

Turnover Can Be a Good Thing

Turnover isn't always bad—in fact, when you are getting rid of low-performing salespeople, it's good. We recommend replacing the bottom 20 percent of your sales force every year. We know this sounds cold, but the fact is that those people just aren't working out as part of your team. They will be happier and more productive in another environment, and your company will be in better shape with different people.

Jack Welch, former CEO of General Electric and a best-selling author, calls this the principle of differentiation. He calls for replacing the bottom 10 percent of your entire workforce every year. He says the concept is based on the fact that the team with the best players wins. Professional sports teams know this well—it's why they replace the bottom of their rosters every year. While 10 percent may be the most effective number on an overall basis, we think that 20 percent is more appropriate for your sales team.

If you refer back to the focus chart on page 61 in Strategy Four, you'll see that salespeople in the bottom 20 percent are focused on survival and just making quota. You want salespeople who are focused on excelling, who want to go beyond the minimum, and who are excited about what they're doing. If after you have done everything you reasonably can to move those low performers up they are still in the bottom 20 percent, it's time to make a change. Let them go elsewhere while you use Strategies One and Two to find people who will produce at a higher level.

Will you always have a bottom 20 percent? Of course. But the benefit of replacing them every year is that your overall scale moves up. The bottom 20 percent on your team this year will perform better than the bottom 20 percent did last year or the year before. And that pushes the performance of everyone up.

KEY LESSONS

* Sales managers need to know how to give feedback that results in continuous improvement; how to provide ongoing

training in the form of classes, coaching, and discussion; and how to handle joint sales calls for maximum effectiveness.

✳ Meaningful feedback is done in real time, immediately following the sales call. Give feedback in a positive manner, suggesting changes when appropriate, but never in a belittling or insulting way.

✳ Make sure your sales team has access to ongoing classes, ongoing coaching, discussions about successes and failures, and joint calls with the sales manager and other salespeople.

✳ Joint calls are your best coaching tool. Set expectations and call objectives, then evaluate how the call went as soon as you're finished.

✳ Replace the bottom 20 percent of your sales force every year.

Gain and Sustain Momentum

Building and sustaining momentum on your sales team means the difference between a flash in the pan and reaching a true flashpoint. The way to do that is to establish a cycle of proven strategies and keep doing them: Recruit and hire the right people, give them the tools they need, establish expectations, measure results, train, coach, and provide feedback and course correction. It's simple, especially once you have a system, but it takes effort and commitment.

Principles of Motivation

As we have said, motivation comes from within. You cannot motivate someone else. But what you can do is create an environment in which people find it easy to motivate themselves.

Motivators are the values, concepts, or things that cause a person to take action toward achieving personal and professional goals. Here's what you need to understand about motivation:

· *People are motivated by different things.* Some people are motivated by money and material gain. Others are motivated by recognition. Still others are motivated by being able to spend time with family and friends or by opportunities to serve. To create a culture that will motivate your sales team and lead to momentum, take the time to understand and respect what motivates each individual.

· *Motivation comes from within.* You cannot motivate someone else; all you can do is create the proper environment for self-motivation to occur. We've said this before—we can't stress it enough. It is not your responsibility to motivate others; they are responsible for themselves. But it is your responsibility to make it as easy as possible for them to stay motivated.

· *What is important to you may not be important to others.* Just as people are motivated by different things, they also value different things. It's not right or wrong, good or bad, it just is. Learn to understand and accept it.

· *People need short, medium, and long-range goals to keep them focused and directed.* It's hard to get motivated if you don't have goals. And reaching a goal—or at least a designated milestone on the way to a goal—is a tremendous motivator to keep going. As you coach your people, help them set goals that will be motivating.

· *It's easier to demotivate than it is to motivate.* This is a sad but true fact of human nature. Most people are far

> *"Nothing can stop the man with the right mental attitude from achieving his goal; nothing on earth can help the man with the wrong mental attitude."*
>
> —Thomas Jefferson

quicker to accept "you can't do that" than they are to believe that they can accomplish something they haven't done before. This is why feedback always needs to be done in the most positive terms. One casual, thoughtless comment can outweigh months of careful coaching.

· *A team is only as enthusiastic as you are.* You're the leader; you set the tone.

· *The speed of the lead dog determines the speed of the pack.* How fast do you want your pack to move?

Three Ways to Support Motivation

As a sales manager, you contribute to an environment that is ripe for self-motivation through leadership, management, and supervision. Your leadership shows your team what to do, your management keeps them on track, and your supervision lets them know you care. The goal of strong leadership is to make sure that the right things are done. The goal of good management is to make sure things are done right. Quality supervision combines leadership and management in a way that helps your team know what to do and holds them accountable in a way that is positive and creates an environment in which they are constantly striving to do better. It all works together for a motivated sales team.

Three Key Sales Force Management Issues

The three key issues to manage with your sales force are:

1. *Objectives.* Make sure they have specific, achievable objectives and a plan for reaching those objectives. Track their progress and hold them accountable for their performance.

> *"Never tell people how to do things. Tell them what to do and they will surprise you with their ingenuity."*
>
> —General George Smith Patton Jr.

What Do Top Performers Want?

How do you create an environment that is ideal for retaining top performers? Simple: Give them what they want. You'll find that what top sales performers want is probably going to be good for your entire company. And even though every salesperson is unique with different motivations and approaches to reaching their goals, there are still some wants they have in common.

- *Accountability*. Top performers want to be held accountable for what they do. They do it well, and they know it. They want to be sure you know it, too.

- *To be part of a high-performance team*. Top performers want to be among other top performers because they are competitive and crave the challenge. They feed on one another's energy. They don't want to be the lead dog if everybody else is a mile behind; they want to be the lead dog when everybody is packed tightly together and the second- and third-place holders are chasing them.

- *Meaningful education and training*. Top performers want to be learning things relevant to their work so they can continue to improve—but don't waste their time with programs they can't or won't use.

- *Proper tools*. Top performers want to be provided with the tools necessary to perform in the culture in which they are operating.

- *Authority equal to responsibility*. Top performers want responsibility, but they also want the authority to make decisions at the appropriate level.

- *Recognition*. Top performers want recognition for their achievements and position as a top performer.

- *A defined career path*. Top performers are goal-oriented, and they want to know what's next. They don't like surprises in this area.

2. *Behavior.* How they act needs to be consistent both with what is necessary to reach their goals as well as your culture.

3. *Values.* Know what's important to each member of your team so you can help them motivate themselves.

Myths about Top Performers

Don't buy into these popular myths about top performers:

- *They are all prima donnas and require prima-donna treatment.* Some are and do, but most are not and do not.

- *They don't need coaching.* All salespeople need coaching, and your top performers can benefit from it as much, and probably more, than your low performers. In fact, top performers often demand it because they want to get even better than they already are.

- *They are difficult to manage.* If you are demonstrating strong leadership and have taken the time to get to know them as individuals, they are no more difficult to manage than any professional.

- *They are all good account managers.* Some are, some aren't. They're individuals.

- *They all want to become sales managers.* Most would be very unhappy as sales managers, and many of them realize they are better off as senior salespeople.

- *They are no longer motivated by money.* Motivators rarely change. Even if they don't need money, if they have been motivated by money in the past, they will continue to be, because it represents achievement.

- *They don't want to be part of the team.* They do want to be part of the team but on their terms.

Focus on Your Top and Middle Performers

There is a common tendency among companies to focus their attentions on the low performers to try to bring them up. That

approach might have value in school where the mission is education, but it isn't effective in the workplace, especially with salespeople, where the mission is running a profitable business. When
you put too much effort and energy in your bottom 20 percent at
the expense of others, you pull the top performers down.

Look at it from the perspective of the top performer, who is
likely to think: "I'm working hard, I'm doing things right, I'm producing results—and I'm being ignored. The people who are getting
the attention are the screwups."

You don't want to ignore anybody on your team, but consider
the return on investment. Let's say you have someone who is in the
bottom 20 percent. You send him to training, you spend time
coaching him, you do other thing to encourage him, and maybe
you can boost him up a few points—just far enough up so that he
doesn't get fired. Now think about what someone who is in the
top 20 percent would do if you did the same type of training,
coaching, and encouraging. Do you think that person's performance just might shoot off the charts? And the people in the middle just might give your top performers a run for their money if
they're given some additional support.

In Strategy Fourteen, we talked about replacing the bottom 20
percent of your sales team every year. This is a sound business
strategy. You're not in school, this isn't a civic group or a church,
it's a business. And as a business, you need salespeople who are
selling, not salespeople who are struggling.

We are not suggesting that you pick an arbitrary date and fire
everyone who is in the bottom 20 percent on that day. But if you
have 50 salespeople, over the course of a year, you should replace
10 of them. If you are communicating with them, and they know
their performance is not acceptable, most will simply leave on
their own. They'll see the handwriting on the wall and leave
before they get fired. And chances are, if they are in the bottom 20
percent, they aren't happy working for you anyway. You're doing

them a favor by encouraging them to go somewhere else.

At JK Harris & Company, we are very candid with our sales team. We tell them that if they stay in the bottom 20 percent for any length of time, they will be terminated. We do whatever we can do to help them, but we're not going to let people who are draining our resources do that indefinitely. We believe that's in the best interest of the company as well as the best interest of the other salespeople.

> *"You get the best effort from others not by lighting a fire beneath them, but by building a fire within."*
> —Bob Nelson

Don't Let the Top Performers Hold You Hostage

While we firmly believe in respecting and nurturing your top performers, we also think that their conduct should be reciprocal. There is no one so great that you can't do without him. Don't let your top performers get away with breaking rules or doing anything else that could harm your company.

At JK Harris & Company, we have two sales consultants who are head and shoulders above the rest in the rankings and have been for years. We respect them, we appreciate them, and we reward them. But not long ago, one of them did something that was a serious conflict of interest. The only reason he wasn't fired was because I didn't want to do that to his family. He's contributed a lot to the company, and it was the first mistake he'd made—but it was serious. So instead of firing him, I suspended him without pay for two weeks, and he knows that if he pulls a stunt like that again, he will be fired. We did not make a public announcement about this, but the news spread through the company like wildfire. Everybody knows that we will not tolerate that sort of conduct from anyone, even top producers.

Don't let the tail wag the dog. Your top performers are valuable, but they still have to play by the rules. If you let them get

> *"I can't put in you what
> nature left out."*
> —JK Harris

away with breaking the rules, your sales force will lose respect for you, the rest of your management team, and the company in general. Don't tolerate anything from your top performers that you wouldn't tolerate from anyone else—and never tolerate deliberate misconduct.

Sales Management Mistakes that Will Block Momentum

Be aware of these mistakes and monitor yourself to avoid them:

- *Giving automatic sales quota increases based on previous performance.* Quota increases should be based on a comprehensive review of the territory, market conditions, salesperson's skill level, company's product line changes, and anything else that might affect performance.
- *Too many contests.* Keep the focus on professional sales, not contests.
- *Not taking salespeople to task when necessary.* When they make mistakes, deal with it, don't ignore it. They're adults, they can handle it.
- *Not soliciting ideas from salespeople.* Your salespeople have a unique perspective based on how they interact with your customers. Let them tell you how you can improve the company.
- *Not valuing your salespeople's opinions.* When members of your sales team express their thoughts and ideas, respond with respect and consider their input thoughtfully.
- *Failing to implement good ideas when they are solicited.* Worse than failing to solicit ideas is to ask for them and then ignore them. If you get a good idea, implement it. If the idea isn't good or won't work, let the salesperson know why.

- *Taking experienced salespeople for granted.* Just because they're good and they've been around for years doesn't mean they'll stay if they feel unappreciated.
- *Bragging about your latest "find" or next sales superstar.* Don't say things that will make your existing team feel like they're second-rate.
- *Failing to recognize or appreciate the role your salespeople's spouses play in their lives and their work.* Look for ways to let the significant others know that their support is appreciated and valued.
- *Not knowing the names, hobbies, interests, etc., of your salespeople's children.* This is part of getting to know your reps as individuals—their families are a key part of who they are.
- *Assuming you can continually motivate salespeople with money.* People have different and multiple motivators. It's not always money, and even when it is money, it's usually not only money.
- *Expecting salespeople to automatically embrace technology, new products, or change.* Many people don't like change and will actively resist it, even when they logically understand that it's for the better.
- *Believing salespeople will submit paperwork, reports, or other required items without prodding or consequences if they don't comply.* Most salespeople find the paperwork a tedious necessary evil and will ignore it if you let them get away with it.

Raise the Bar Every Day

Always be recruiting salespeople, even when you don't have an opening. That gives you a pool of prequalified candidates to turn to when an opening occurs.

Finally, maintain accountability and look for every opportunity that will allow people to stretch, to compete with their own personal best. Never be satisfied with the status quo.

—— **KEY LESSONS** ——

✳ Understand the principles of motivation. People are motivated by different things. Motivation comes from within. What is important to one may not be important to someone else. People need short, medium, and long-range goals. It's easier to de-motivate than it is to motivate. A team is only as enthusiastic as its leader.

✳ Support motivation on your team through leadership, management, and supervision.

✳ The three key issues to manage with your sales team are objectives, behavior, and values.

✳ Top performers want accountability, to be part of a high-performance team, meaningful education and training, proper tools, authority equal to responsibility, recognition, and a defined career path.

✳ You'll get a better return on investment if you focus your training and coaching efforts on you middle and top performers, rather than the bottom 20 percent.

✳ Never let a top performer hold you hostage. No one is so great that you can't do without him. Don't let your top performers get away with breaking rules or otherwise harming your company.

✳ Sales management mistakes that will block momentum include automatic sales quote increases based on previous performance, too many contests, not taking salespeople to task when necessary, not soliciting ideas from salespeople, failing to implement ideas when they are solicited, taking experienced salespeople for granted, and not appreciating the role spouses and families play in a salesperson's work.

Reaching the Flashpoint

The sales management role is crucial to the ultimate success of any organization. The largest issue facing companies today in terms of performance, meeting goals, maintaining high levels of activity, and achieving sales objectives is far more attributable to the effectiveness of the sales manager than it is to the salespeople.

Most salespeople are not getting sufficient attention and guidance from their managers. If you think that top performers want to be left alone to do their jobs, you are wrong. The reality is that they crave attention. They want help. They want mentoring. They want to be recognized. Most of all, they want a resource they can go to that they trust to help them maintain and improve their level of performance. That resource should be the sales manager—and when it is, you've reached the Sales Flashpoint.

About JK Harris

JK (John) Harris is the quintessential entrepreneur: an astute leader with tremendous business acumen who's always on the lookout for new opportunities. After holding senior management positions in a number of companies, he went on to found or purchase 18 businesses in his 30-year business career—and has plans for more.

The son of a schoolteacher and a federal government employee, John grew up on a dairy farm in rural South Carolina, which introduced him to a wide range of important business fundamentals at an early age. He attended Carlisle Military School in Bamberg, South Carolina, where he played basketball and baseball, developed his leadership skills, and graduated as salutatorian of his class. Continuing his education, he worked full time while attending the University of South Carolina, graduating *cum laude* with a degree in history and political science in 1976. He went on to earn his master's in accounting in 1977.

His first post-college job was as a staff accountant at Haskins & Sells, CPAs (now Deloitte Touche Tohmatsu) in Charlotte, North Carolina. During his 13 months with that firm, John achieved an important accomplishment and made a critical self-discovery: He received his Certified Public Accountant certificate and realized he was far better suited to being a CPA's client than a CPA. He launched his entrepreneurial career, and never looked back.

Over the years, he has been the founder, owner, or co-owner of businesses in a range of industries, including automotive and construction, as well as business, consumer and professional services. He is, by his own admission, a serial entrepreneur. He's also easily bored, and that's what drives him to constantly seek new challenges.

John opened his accounting practice in 1996 to share his business expertise with other entrepreneurs in the Charleston area. When a new accounting client came to him owing the IRS $90,000, John was able to settle it for $42,000. In the process, he realized that there was a dearth of qualified assistance for taxpayers who were in debt to the IRS. He decided that JK Harris & Company would focus on those services and in 1997 decided to grow his two-person accounting practice into the nation's largest tax representation firm. In less than five years, JK Harris & Company went from a single office to 325 offices in 43 states with annual revenues of more than $100 million. Today, JK Harris & Company continues to lead the tax representation and small business services industry, and John continues to serve as president and CEO of the firm.

Crediting much of his success to lessons learned from other entrepreneurs as well as his own experience, John Harris has made it his mission to share his knowledge and expertise with business

owners and managers across the country and throughout the world through his books and speeches. In 2009, he wrote his first book, *Flashpoint: Seven Core Strategies for Rapid-Fire Business Growth.* That was followed by *Sales Flashpoint: Fifteen Strategies for Rapid-Fire Sales Growth*, and he is currently working on the next book in the Flashpoints series, along with a series of teleseminars and e-books.

As the founder and Fire Chief of Flashpoints Consulting, LLC, John Harris is committed to serving as a resource for entrepreneurs who want to grow bigger, stronger, and more profitable companies.

About Richard D. Dickerson

R ichard D. Dickerson is a consummate sales professional who learned his craft the hard way and has dedicated himself to smoothing the path for others. Richard's understanding and appreciation for sales and entrepreneurship began at an early age as he grew up watching his father run the family commercial painting business that had been founded by his great-grandfather. Painting didn't appeal to him, but he was intrigued by the sales process.

After graduating with a BA in Economics from Virginia Tech, Richard spent five years teaching high school math and algebra in Tappahannock, Virginia, a small town between Richmond and Washington, DC. As many teachers do, he worked at a nonteaching job in the summers; he sold tractors, feed, seed, and farm implements. He realized what he loved was selling. Filled with hope and optimism but without much in the way of prospects, he left teaching

and found a company willing to take a chance on a rookie sales rep in a straight commission position traveling the southeastern United States.

During his first year, Richard became a master at dealing with rejection. Then he had the good fortune of acquiring a mentor, a man with 40-plus years of selling success who was willing to share what he knew and guide his young protégé. By year three, Richard knew that he was doing what he was meant to do—and doing it well. For the next 25 years, he prospered as a manufacturer's rep.

Then he met Bill Brooks (William T. Brooks, the man to whom *Sales Flashpoint* is dedicated), a speaker, consultant, author, and CEO of his sales training company. Impressed and inspired by Bill's approach to business, Richard joined The Brooks Group in 1995. As the company's national accounts manager, Richard continues to sell, consult, and facilitate with clients around the country. He takes immense personal pride in helping identify and develop top sales talent for his clients and in the process of doing that continues to develop his own skills and professional abilities. He has never forgotten his first mentor, the man who was able to recognize his own raw talent and show him how to grow into the industry leader he is today.

In 2010, Richard D. Dickerson teamed up with JK Harris, who is both a client and friend, to write *Sales Flashpoint: Fifteen Strategies for Rapid-Fire Sales Growth*, where both men share the wisdom they have gained so readers can quickly take their own sales teams to the Sales Flashpoint.

Index

Flashpoint: Seven Core Strategies for Rapid-Fire Business Growth

JK Harris tells you how to get to the Flashpoint, the point where your business ignites and launches on a nonstop trajectory toward growth and success.

Harris' seven core strategies were developed through his own experience, refined by trial and error, and can be easily applied to any business of any size in any industry. Available at all major bookstores or online at theflashpoints.com.

Two Free Gifts for You from JK Harris

Thank you for reading *Sales Flashpoint: Fifteen Strategies for Rapid-Fire Sales Growth*. As an expression of his appreciation, JK Harris has two free gifts for you.

The first is JK Harris' exciting e-book, *The Mindset of High Achievers*. Find out how high achievers think, how their mindset affects what they are able to accomplish, and how you can use the same techniques and strategies to achieve more with far less effort than you ever dreamed possible.

The second is a complimentary subscription to *Flashpoints* newsletter. Get wisdom and information from JK Harris and the Flashpoints team delivered via e-mail. Each month, Flashpoints will bring you timely articles and resources to help you deal with issues related to starting and managing a fast-growing, profitable company—all absolutely free.

Help take your company to the Flashpoint by accepting these two free gifts from JK Harris. Visit theflashpoints.com to claim your gifts today.

flashpoints

Financial Flashpoint:
Strategies for Economic Success

Take your company to its Financial Flashpoint using critical strategies from entrepreneur and business expert JK Harris that cover such vital business issues as:

- Finding capital
- Obtaining loans and dealing with lenders
- Investor relations
- Cash management
- Administration and record-keeping
- Taxes
- Cost controls
- Purchasing
- Risk management
- Credit and collections
- And more, including a special bonus section on personal financial management strategies

Financial Flashpoint: Strategies for Economic Success will be in bookstores October 2011. Subscribe to the Flashpoints newsletter (theflashpoints.com) to be alerted when pre-publication copies are available.

flashpoints

Invite JK Harris to Speak at Your Event

JK (John) Harris is an engaging speaker with a valuable message about how you can take your business to the Flashpoint of growth and profitability. John's dynamic presentations at conferences, conventions, and corporate meetings are designed to entertain, inform, and leave audiences energized, enthused, and looking forward to his next appearance.

JK Harris accepts a limited number of speaking engagements each year. To book him for your event, visit **theflash points.com** today.

THE BROOKS GROUP

About The Brooks Group

Founded in 1977, The Brooks Group is a sales, sales management, and leadership consulting firm that has helped more than 2,000 organizations in 450 industries transform their business practices through practical, down-to-earth skills development in sales, sales management, and leadership growth.

This dedicated group of professionals helps sales-driven organizations build top-producing teams with comprehensive assessment systems, innovative sales and sales management training, and quality consulting services.

The Brooks Group builds and sustains top-performing business development programs and effective, productive personnel through a five-step process:

Step 1: Assessment of existing organizations and positions, in-place personnel, and potential hires. Do you have the right people in the right places?

THE BROOKS GROUP

Step 2: Customized solutions to your most serious business development issues. Once you have the right person, how do you work with him or her most effectively?

Step 3: Program delivery of world-class training sessions adapted to your environment. Do your employees need training in sales, sales management, or leadership-related topics?

Step 4: Reinforcement of key concepts via coaching and online and telephone tutoring tools. If you have the right people and have put them on the right track, what next?

Step 5: Measurable accountability mechanisms to track your organization's progress. Do you think you have the right people in the right places? Can you prove it?

The basis of The Brooks Group's training programs is the IMPACT Selling System, a consistent, repeatable sales process based on proven, nonmanipulative principles that is

THE BROOKS GROUP

easy to learn and use. It combines prospecting and selling competencies into one integrated methodology, and enables salespeople to maximize each business opportunity by focusing on the customers and their individual perceptions of value.

Based on best practices and proven sales principles, IMPACT is a framework easily adaptable to any industry, product, or service. In fact, over the past 30 years, The Brooks Group has successfully taught the IMPACT Selling System to more than 500,000 people in the manufacturing/distribution, health-care, and financial services industries, as well as branches of the U.S. military.

The Brooks Group
3810 North Elm St., #202
Greensboro, NC 27455
(800) 633-7762
TheBrooksGroup.com